A BRIEF HISTORY *of*

RAYMOND
NEW HAMPSHIRE

A BRIEF HISTORY *of*

RAYMOND NEW HAMPSHIRE

PAUL BROWN

THE History PRESS

Published by The History Press
Charleston, SC 29403
www.historypress.net

Cover image courtesy of Jean Spillane.

First published 2014

Manufactured in the United States

ISBN 978.1.62619.600.1

Library of Congress CIP data applied for.

CONTENTS

ACKNOWLEDGEMENTS

Many people have contributed to this book. Sally Paradis, the "Editor-in-Chief," was the inspiration for the Raymond Historical Society to write the history of Raymond from the mid-1970s to the present. She has organized the topics of interest and tasked individuals with expertise in the topics with writing the articles.

Paul Brown had been working on a history with a somewhat different flavor with the intent of providing future historians with an insight of Raymond's way of life in the recent past, as well as glimpses into early Raymond history.

With the realization that the two works should be complementary, and not competing, it was decided to combine them into a single book. The History Press, a publisher that specializes in such works, will publish and market the final product, and any royalties will go to the Raymond Historical Society. While Paul Brown is named as the "primary author," the writers of factual details are given attribution as the authors with each section title. "Primary authorship," in this case, meets the requirements of the publisher and is considerably less complicated than any other arrangement.

We thank Joyce Wood and her collection of Raymond postcards, and her tireless efforts for the Raymond Historical Society; Jonathan Wood for his efforts for the Historical Society; and his work in compiling Raymond business information; Leslie O'Donnell as a professional editor; and the others as listed with each article.

INTRODUCTION

The seminal history of Raymond was written by Joseph Fullonton and published in 1875. Fullonton presented a marvelous array of history, anecdotes, genealogy and biographies. His book is a rich source of detail about Raymond's early times.

The 200th anniversary of Raymond's incorporation was in 1964, and that year, Shirley Barnes wrote another history. Mrs. Barnes summarized Fullonton and then added her own account of Raymond happenings from 1875 to 1964.

In 1976, the *Pictorial History of Raymond* was published by the Raymond Historical Society. Finally, in 2008, we have *Images of America: Raymond* by Kristin Ozana Doyle.

Now, in 2014, Raymond will celebrate its 250th* anniversary. From its humble beginning in 1764, and through the work and efforts of so many of its townspeople over the years, Raymond continues to be a great place to call home. Located in a state where the "quality of life" is high on the agenda, Raymond offers much to its people. In 1989, the question was asked: "What will Raymond be like when it celebrates its 250th birthday in 2014?" The answer was "we can only guess."

Our date with destiny has arrived. By no means perfect, Raymond has forged ahead since 1989 into the twenty-first century with much to be

---

*Since the 150th birthday is a sesquicentennial, one might assume this to be the sesqui-bicentennial, but some research on Wikipedia suggests "sestercentennial," "semiquincentennial" and "quarter-millennial." Princeton University used "bicenquinquagenary" in 1996, but what do they know?

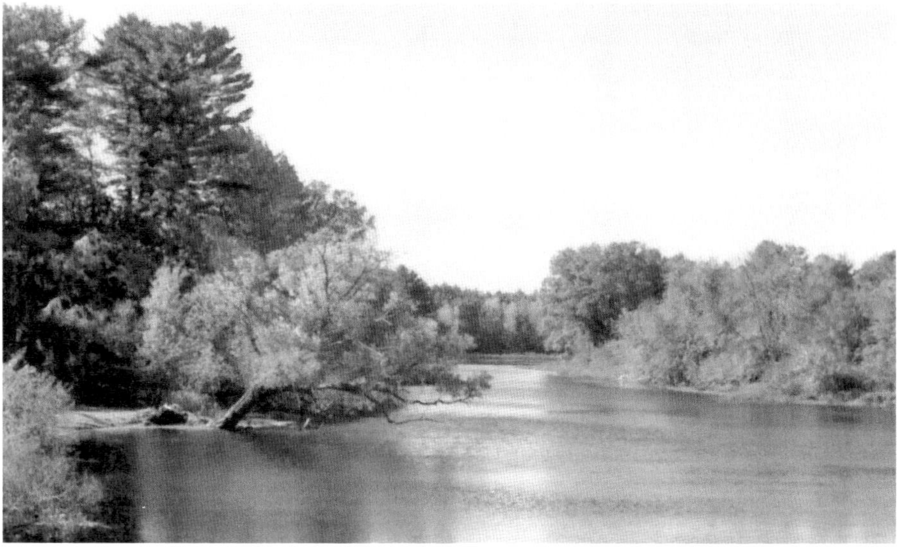

"Fair Raymond, We Love Thee"—A view from Pecker Bridge. *Courtesy of Paul Brown.*

proud of. With a rededication to those ideals that our forefathers sought so many years before, may the words of the 250th celebration slogan—"My Town, Your Town, Our Town"—bring about a new spirit of unity and cooperation for the betterment of our "Fair Raymond."

1

FIRST THINGS FIRST: THE NAME "RAYMOND"

Prior to the town's incorporation in 1764, it was called "Freetown." The reason for this is that the largest pines were supposed to go to the king for use on his majesty's ships as masts. It seems that the locals had other ideas.

The king's agents would hack the letter *R* (for *rex*, Latin for "king") on a tree that they deemed fit for a king. The locals simply ignored the mark and cut the tree for their own use; therefore, so far as they were concerned, this area was a "free town." It makes sense.

The town's preeminent historian, Joseph Fullonton, wrote some 110 years after incorporation that changing the name from "Freetown" to "Raymond" was "taking a new and classical one, [and] shows that there are minds not disposed to tread all the time in one path, but capable of thinking and advancing." Fullonton also avers that *ray* and *monde* mean "shining world."

Fullonton also gives an account of the king's agents seizing a load of timber and running the wagon into the river.

In 1970, Elmer Munson Hunt wrote *New Hampshire Town Names and Whence They Came*, in which he claims that the name "Raymond" was named for a Captain William Rayment, or Raymond, who had raised a company of soldiers to fight in the war against Canada. Land in Raymond, Hunt asserted, was granted to soldiers from Beverly, Massachusetts, and it was also known as Beverly-Canada. He also stated that the town was given an exemption from the tree-cutting rule.

After having read Fullonton as a teenager, I was somewhat surprised at Hunt's revelation but reserved my skepticism; perhaps Hunt knew something I didn't know. But how could he know something Fullonton didn't know, ninety-five years earlier?

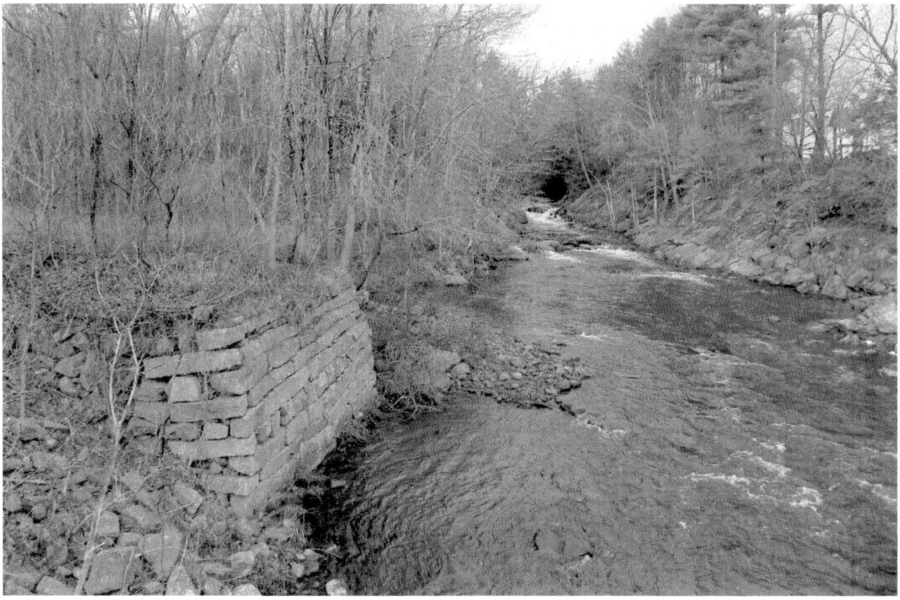

Remains of stonework of Freetown Bridge. *Courtesy of Paul Brown.*

More recently, Matthew Thomas of Fremont, a thorough and knowledgeable historian, confirmed my skepticism with the observation that numerous of Hunt's pronouncements were incorrect or, at least, that there was no discernable evidence supporting his claims.

Further research into the matter and a reading of *History of Old Chester*, by Benjamin Chase, establishes that the original grants in what is now Raymond were to favored families from the New Hampshire seacoast area, and there is no mention of Beverly, Massachusetts, or any soldiers.

So this leads me to guess that the name "Raymond" was probably chosen over "Freetown" at incorporation because "Freetown" might have smacked of outlawry and "Raymond" had a more "classical" ring, as Fullonton's approval implies.

I have seen one transfer of land in Raymond, prior to incorporation, which refers to the Parish of Raymond, in the Township of Chester."

We still have a Freetown Road, which until a few years ago, terminated near the former site of the Freetown Mill, and the area of the first settlement, where the Bean Tavern, site of the first town meetings, still stands.

Now, Freetown Road is also State Routes 107 and 102, running from Route 27 to the junction of Chester and Fremont Roads, where 107 and 102 split. Driving southerly from the Route 101 Exit 5 interchange, and crossing the Lamprey River, one can see the granite slabs of the bridge that crossed the river at this point on the original Freetown Road, and slightly upstream of this is where the very early Freetown Mill was sited.

A bit of Internet research finds the *Yearbook of the Society of Colonial Wars in the Commonwealth of Massachusetts for 1898*, containing acts of the Massachusetts legislature dated 1735 granting land to Captain Rayment's soldiers. The "Raymond" was not in New Hampshire, but in the state of Maine, which was then a part of Massachusetts.

I hate to belabor the point, but it seems highly unlikely that the group of miscreants who was willing to snitch the king's logs and secede from Chester would take kindly to having its town regranted to a bunch of soldiers from Massachusetts.

2

RAYMOND AIN'T NYC

It's early morning, about seven o'clock, late May or early June 1953. The location is in front of Blake's store, which was between Candyland and the Congregational Church.

An eighteen-year-old boy stands apart from a group of chattering teenagers stepping off the interstate bus. They have just returned from their class trip to New York City.

The kid looks across at the Common and is suddenly aware of the contrast between this quiet village and the city of a day earlier. He has seen this lush green triangle from his earliest memories, but never as he does now.

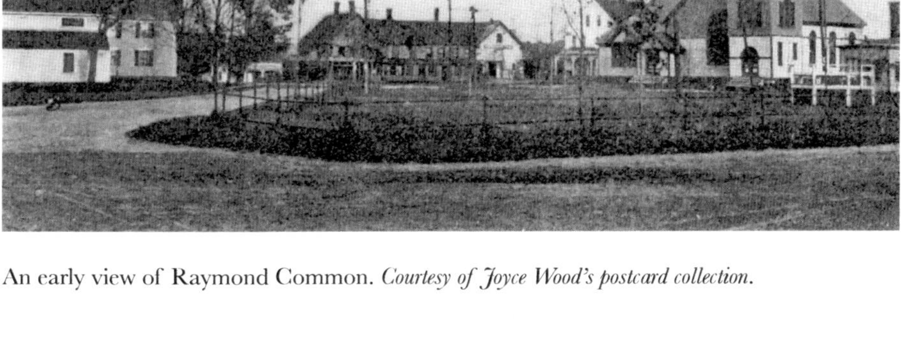

An early view of Raymond Common. *Courtesy of Joyce Wood's postcard collection.*

The late spring pastel green of the maples softens the sunlight, the landscape is soothing—there *is* a landscape, so much more to see in every leaf and every blade of grass than in the concrete and steel and sharp angles of the city.

The village the kid sees is of wooden houses, the fire station, the library.

There's a statue in the Common, a quiet, gray sentinel standing guard over a peaceful village. The class was up in the crown of the Statue of Liberty the other day, grimy with the graffiti of a thousand tourists. Somehow, this warrior is friendlier than the one that was meant to welcome immigrants.

Too often we talk about defining moments, but this may have been one. The kid—who would be me—had always seen the same scruffy little village, winter and summer. Now I am comparing it with the stark city streets, the tall, overwhelming buildings occupied by millions of unknown souls.

Here, my eyes found such peace and tranquility in those soft, watercolor-green maples. This heretofore homely place was home.

3

BUSINESS AND PROFESSIONAL WORLDS

Surveys were sent to all known businesses in Raymond, complete with self-addressed stamped envelopes. Very few were returned. The effort was followed by telephone calls to the largest employers and a notice in the two online news publishers.

Responding Businesses

Ace Hardware/Ben Franklin

Richard & Karen Vinson, forty-three employees
Raymond Shopping Center, 15 Freetown Road, Raymond, New Hampshire
Grand Opening February 1973
We believe it is our responsibility to provide a complete selection of quality merchandise to satisfy our customers' needs in hardware, variety and crafts at competitive prices. We strive to provide the best customer services in a pleasant shopping atmosphere.

Access Sports Medicine & Orthopaedics

Joshua Siegel, MD, and Roderick Bruno, MD, fifteen employees
We are a full-service orthopaedic and sports medicine physician's office. We offer physical and occupational therapy, work injury treatment, occupational medicine, digital X-ray services, open MRI, concussion management, ultrasound and more.

Andrew J. Harmon, Attorney at Law

Andrew J. Harmon, four employees
Raymond, Manchester & Concord
Established 1997
Law office.

Beneficial Bodyworks

Tina Graham, three employees
151 Route 27, Raymond, New Hampshire
Established March 2007
As a wellness-based company, we are committed to our mission of providing the highest level of customer care in a safe and comfortable environment, making a positive impact on our community and offering quality alternative therapies and services.

BJ Carpet Services

Robert P. Bracket
154 Route 27, Raymond, New Hampshire
July 1974—Opened Present Showroom April 1984
Flooring Sales & Installations, Including: Carpet, Vinyl Floors, Laminate & Pre-Finished Hardwood Floors

Blocks to Books Children's Center

Kellie Jewett, eight employees
129 Route 27, Raymond, New Hampshire
Established October 1995
Blocks to Books Children's Center is a full-service childcare and early childhood education facility, providing a safe, caring, educational and fun environment for children in the Greater Raymond Area.

Cornerstone Physical Therapy Associates, LLC

Denise Simard, PT, six employees
64 Freetown Road, Raymond, New Hampshire
Established September 2006
Our mission is to be at the forefront of the rehabilitation industry, providing exceptional one-on-one care through the continuum of recovery and prevention.

Crayon Campus

Linda Priebe, two employees
64 Freetown Road, Unit B, Raymond, New Hampshire
Established October 2006
Our philosophy is that childhood is a time like no other, a time for exploring, socializing, discovering and creating.

Creative Classrooms

Fritz Bell, two employees
81 Chester Rd, Raymond, NH
Established October 1972
Our mission is to provide hands-on training in the creative arts to educators of all levels for use in their classrooms.

Elliot Pediatrics and Primary Care at Raymond

Elliot Hospital
15 Freetown Road, Raymond, New Hampshire
Established 2001
Elliot Hospital, a leader in healthcare, is dedicated to providing its community with excellent services offered with dignity, caring and respect.

Excel Physical Therapy

Jason Garon, three employees
135 Route 27, Raymond, New Hampshire
Established November 2007
Our mission is to enhance the overall physical health, fitness and quality of life for our patients by treating and educating them with high quality, individualized physical therapy services.

Gemini Valve

Daniel Packard, fifty-five employees
2 Otter Court, Raymond, New Hampshire
Established 1974
Our mission is to design and manufacture specialty industrial valves, valve actuators and accessories.

Goodheart Media Services

Marc Vadeboncoeur, two employees
171 Route 27, Raymond, New Hampshire
Established March 2011
We are a leading provider of video production, editing, duplication and media transfer services in northern New England and beyond.

Gordon B. Snyder, Attorney at Law

Gordon B. Snyder
67 Route 27, Raymond, New Hampshire
Established August 1976
Personal legal services for a reasonable price.

Hannaford Brothers Supermarket

Freetown Road
150 Employees
Food and drugstore.

I.C. Reed & Sons, Inc.

Carl B. Reed & Shawn E. Reed, forty employees
8–9 Evans Drive, Raymond, New Hampshire
Established July 1953
Construction, installation, maintenance and repair of overhead and underground medium- and high-voltage power lines, substations, control houses and equipment for public and private utilities, industrial and commercial customers.

Jackson Lumber & Millwork

Torrisi Family, seventy-seven employees
10 Industrial Drive, Raymond, New Hampshire
Company Founded 1946 in Lawrence, Massachusetts; Raymond Facility opened in 2003
We are a manufacturing facility of windows and doors that offers lumber and building materials, as well as a small retail store.

JCR Construction Company, Inc.

Joseph & Christopher Reed, seventy-seven employees
181 Route 27, Raymond, New Hampshire
Established April 1984
Our mission is to provide quality utility construction support for our customers safely and efficiently while maintaining a professional, environmentally friendly workplace.

Jewett Construction Co., Inc.

Craig Jewett, twenty-seven employees
68A Route 27, PO Box 405, Raymond, New Hampshire
Established 1972
Through honesty, openness and communication, we at Jewett Construction Co., Inc., provide professional contracting services with an unparalleled emphasis placed on quality, timeliness, safety and the creation of value for each and every project.

Lilly Jack Photography

Katharine Tristaino Brooks
www.LilyJackPhoto.com
As we all know, some moments are fleeting and can be here and gone in a wink of an eye, but a click of the camera can capture that moment for a lifetime.

Onway Wood Working

Jonathan N. Wood
11 Forest Rd, Raymond, New Hampshire
Etablished January 1997
Creating solutions for your fine woodworking needs.

Paul Brown & Co.

Valuation Services
Long Hill, Raymond, New Hampshire
Over fifty years of real estate valuation expertise.

The Pines Seafood House

Norman & Ann Launier, fifteen to twenty-five employees
171 Route 27, Raymond, New Hampshire
Motto: Treat customers in such a way that they want to return. Quality, quantity, cleanliness and service, all at a great price.

Raymond Animal Hospital

Dr. Steven and Debra Puderbaugh, nine employees
Started at 68 Main Street, Raymond, New Hampshire, May 1985
Opened at 169 Route 27, October 1989
Providing high-quality veterinary care to the town of Raymond and surrounding communities since 1985. We focus on providing client education in the prevention of diseases, quality medical and surgical services and outstanding care for our patients.

Raymond Chiropractic Clinic

Dr. Gary Graham, three employees
151 Route 27, Raymond, New Hampshire
The purpose of this office is to help as many people as possible regain their health by addressing the true cause of disease, not just the symptoms, and to help them maintain their health so that they then, in turn, educate others on the benefits of wellness care.

Raymond Septic Tank Service, LLC

Richard A. Hammond, two employees
11 Old Batchelder Road, Raymond, New Hampshire
Established 1999
Septic systems: design, install, pump.

W.J. Stewart Insurance Agency

William J Stewart, six employees
10 Freetown Road, Raymond, New Hampshire
Established May 1990
Stewart Ltd/Insurance Management was conceived with a specific goal: to operate in a way contrary to traditional insurance agencies. Our approach to both business and personal insurance will be hands-on, one-on-one contact with the customer. The agency will only write that amount of business that can be serviced by an agency owner.

Walnut Hill Conference Center

Fritz Bell, two employees
81 Chester Road, Raymond, New Hampshire
Established June 1974
A conference and retreat center with function rooms and overnight accommodations available for a variety of events.

Walmart Distribution Center

Eight hundred employees
Freetown Road, Raymond, New Hampshire
Established 1996
Saving people money so they can live better.

Web-Kare

Knute Klefos, Mary Ann Wells, Adam Wells, co-owners
74 Main Street, Raymond, New Hampshire
Established July 2000
Our mission is to provide clients with a functional and targeted website that produces sales.

Stores and Shopping, a Look Back

The village was the center of commerce for a century and a half as a stop for the railroad. Some years after the internal combustion engine made its debut, Route 101 was constructed around the village in the late 1930s. Soon after World War II, the first business to settle on the new highway was Daniel A. Sundeen Lumber Company, operated by Daniel Sundeen. Later, it was taken over by Lumbertown. Its latest incarnation has been as a discount store. To my knowledge, there have been three owner/users of that building as of this writing.

Mr. Sundeen, incidentally, developed the street known as Sun Hill just opposite his store.

The Raymond Shopping Center was begun in 1971. Prior to that time, the major grocery store in town was Prescott Farms, located in the former Bourque Shoe Company building, now apartments, behind the historical society building. Prescott's moved to the new shopping center. The state liquor store followed in a separate building, and then the Exeter Banking Company, now Citizens Bank, arrived. Raymond Drug, operated by Frank Case and Jack Ross, moved here from the village. Raymond Drug was eventually bought out by Rite-Aid, which moved to its present building.

Commercial activity followed the Raymond Shopping Center, moving west along Freetown Road and Route 27. Hannaford's was one of the first, then known as Shop 'n' Save. The introduction of this new grocery company resulted in the demise of Prescott Farms in Raymond.

The Cozy Corner complex has a varied history. In the 1940s, it was a store and gas station owned by the Wheadons. Some time in the 1950s, it was purchased by John Peoples, who also operated an antique shop. This operation became a landmark for many years for the beachgoing public before Route 101 was completed. One of the visual attractions was an Italian gondola set on a couple of sawhorses, along with an amazing volume of odd things.

Sadly, two antique homes were demolished to make way for the Irving station and the combined Walgreen's and Advance Auto buildings.

Irving replaced the Houle homestead,* which had a farm stand; the other was the Byron Littlefield home, which had been a chicken farm. I helped to hay the field where the Advance Auto building is now located, and there was a frog pond lying along the highway. That "environmentally sensitive area" is now under many tons of fill elevating the parking area above the street. Personally, I would say that I miss the hayfield, but not the mosquitoes, so I suppose it's a draw.

Diners, Restaurants and the Old Roadhouses

I don't think any of the past historians have mentioned the interesting restaurants, cabins, diners and what one might call a "roadhouse."

In 1934, when Prohibition ended, a couple of these opened for weekend partying, dancing and drinking.

I can remember two of them specifically, one located at Onway Lake, run by the Berry family and housed in their old barn. There were hardwood dance floors, coolers and a bar. It was a busy place on a Saturday night.

Another was located in a barn in Deerfield, less than a mile beyond the town line. It was owned by a person by the name or nickname of Bambino and was known as Bam's Inn. Mr. Bambino later lived in Raymond.

There was a little restaurant in the house adjacent to Dave's Small Engine Repair. This was known as Sunset Camps, and it had a number of little cabins set in a semicircle behind the house. This type of hostelry preceded the modern-day motor courts and motels. It was owned by Mary and Tom Welch. Mr. Welch operated a service garage there.

Radio Grove was a popular spot during the '30s and '40s, where Radio Grove Hardware is located now. It was owned by the Vergos family, and I believe that there were several cabins there. The present building is a newer one built on the old footprint.

The name Radio Grove is believed to have come from the fact that the owners were the first to have a radio and played it over a loudspeaker for their customers.

---

*Hazel Littlefield writes that the Houle home was a "stagecoach inn."

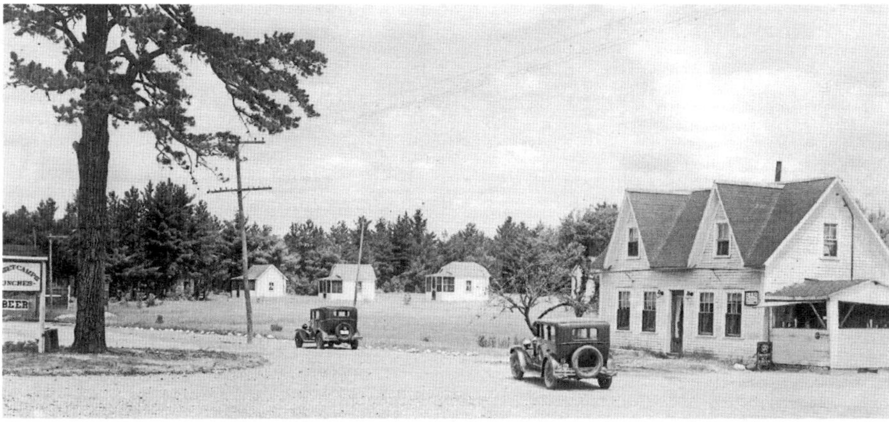

Sunset Camps. *Courtesy of Joyce Wood's postcard collection.*

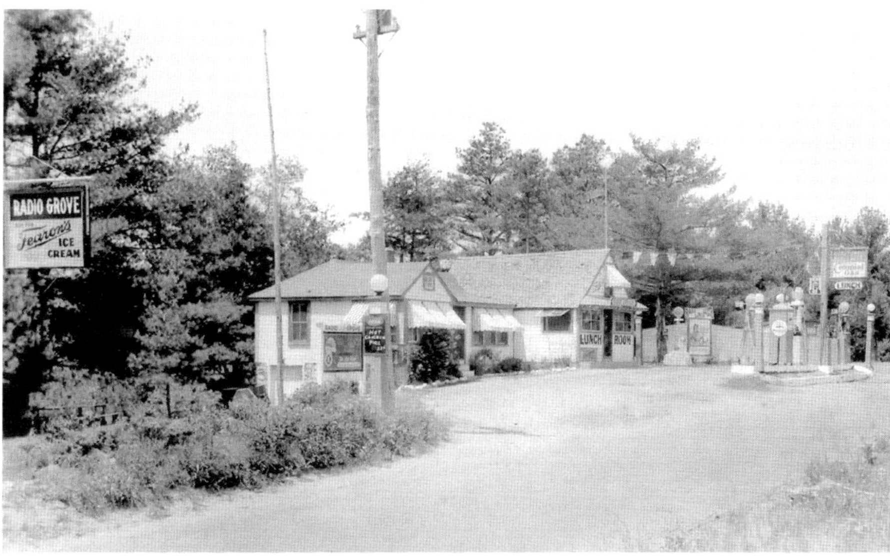

Radio Grove. *Courtesy of Joyce Wood's postcard collection.*

There was a little diner called Glenna's Truck Stop attached to a residence at the west end of Long Hill Road. It may have been the Soup Bowl before that. The house was an old Cape Cod style that had been the home of a Captain Scott, who was the person who subdivided the lots on Scotland Drive. The house and diner were razed in the 1990s. Interestingly, the house may have been a tavern operated by Joseph Dudley as early as 1793. Fullonton describes it as being on the "main road two miles west of the center, where Thomas M. Healey lives." An old map shows a T.M. Healey in this location.

Another hostelry was known as Cold Spring Grove and was located where the storage facility is now situated, across the road from McCusker Lane and the Riverview Manor condos. There were several cabins there, as well as a restaurant.

After the cabins were gone, the restaurant was operated by a number of owners, and its last incarnation was known as the Tailgate restaurant. The Tailgate was a typical roadhouse with country bands on the weekends, and fisticuffs on occasion. It was a lively spot.

Few people will remember Whispering Pines, a little restaurant located across from Lake Carroll. It was owned and operated by Charles and Anna Stickney. I have an old movie of a high school group entering its door.

Then there was Jack's Grill, which is now the westerly end of the building housing Excel Physical Therapy, located across from Lamprey Health Care. This establishment was in business during the 1950s. Sally Paradis told me that you could buy two hot dogs for a quarter.

A diner called Milty and Etta's, operated (oddly enough) by Milton and Etta Margaritis, was located behind the Cumberland Farms store* at the corner of Epping Street and Route 27.

Dinty's Diner, operated by the Surette family, was located in the driveway of Bourque's Shoe, now apartments, near the historical society building.

Another one, Duke's Diner, was located in the large yard to the left of Scott's Barber Shop, across the street from the historical society.

The Long Branch is probably the oldest continually operating restaurant in Raymond. It was a longtime occupant of the building that now houses Supreme House of Pizza. Prior to the Long Branch, the building was a restaurant and beer joint operated by the Tobias family. It had the reputation of being near the location of one of Raymond's few murders. Later, it was owned by the Sansouci family.

The restaurant was operated for many years under the Long Branch name by the Cote twins, Polly Piper and Gerry Mataragas. Gerry did the waitressing, and Polly did the cooking. By most standards, it was a bit grimy (to put it charitably), but the homely meals were inexpensive and filling. It was a genuine piece of Americana. You would see little

---

* The Cumberland Farms store (now closed) was a service garage in the 1940s.

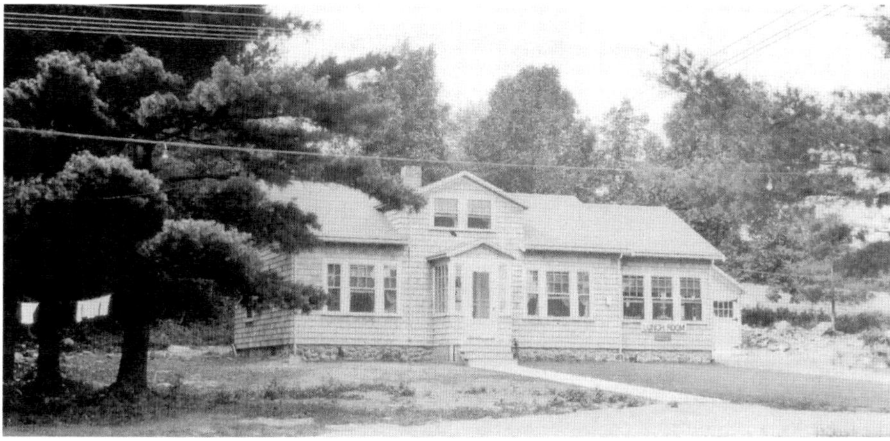

Whispering Pines. *Courtesy of Joyce Wood's postcard collection.*

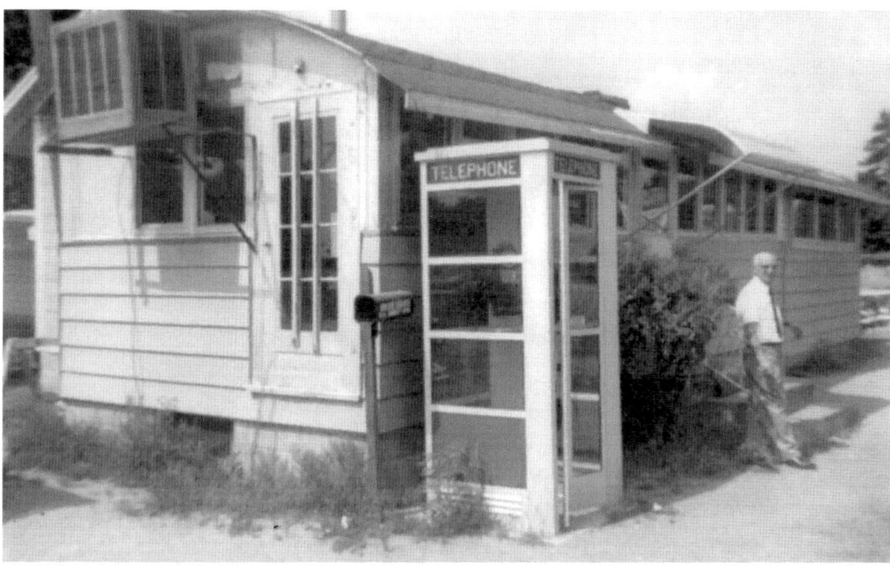

Milty and Etta's Diner. *Courtesy of Leona Margaritis Jean.*

old ladies at the bar with thirty-five-cent beers at eight o'clock in the morning. There was a mounted buck's head on the wall with a marijuana cigarette dangling from its lips.

The business went through a series of owners and moved across the street to its present location.

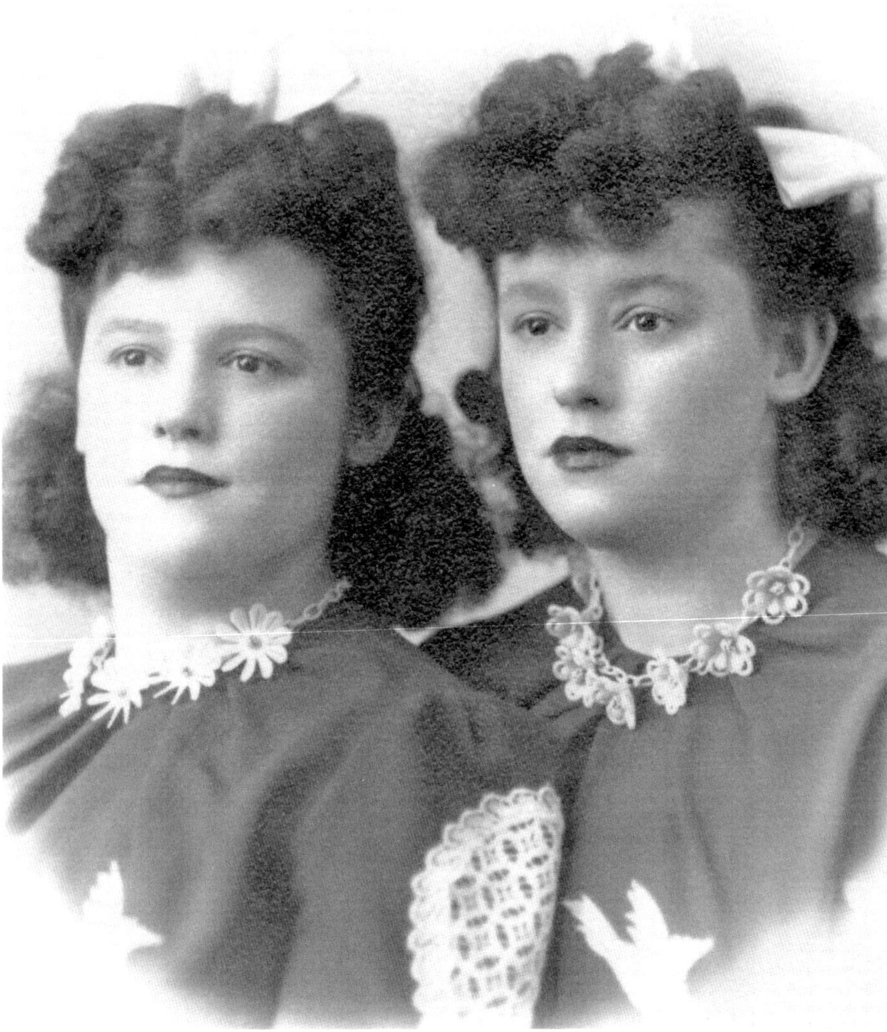

A high school photo of Pauline and Geraldine Cote, proprietors of the Long Branch restaurant. *Courtesy of Chris Mataragas.*

Earlier, in the '40s, Hazel's (Pellerin) Diner was located under an awning of sorts at the Fruit Store. This was a classic that had red stained-glass windows featuring presidents along the driveway side. All of this building burned in the late 1990s.

In the 1940s, for a short time, there was a little restaurant on the left side of Blake's store, which is now an empty space between the Congregational Church and the former Candyland.

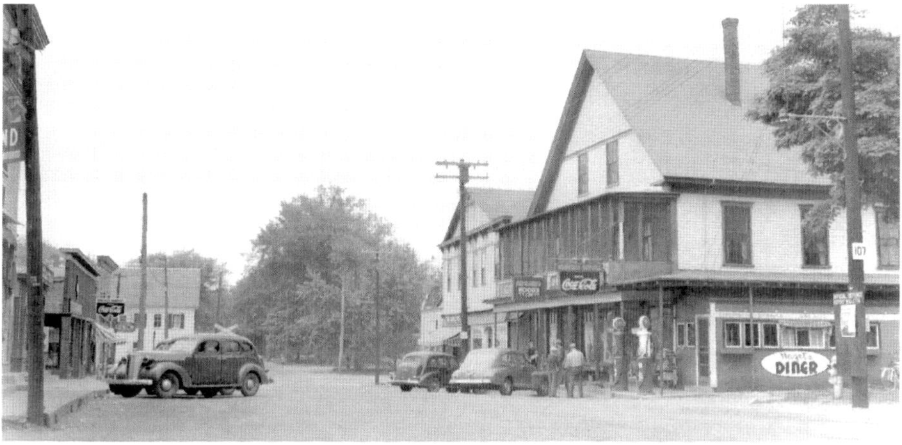

Hazel's Diner (right). Note the "Official Defence [*sic*] Report Bulletin" attached to the pole at right. *Courtesy of Joyce Wood's postcard collection.*

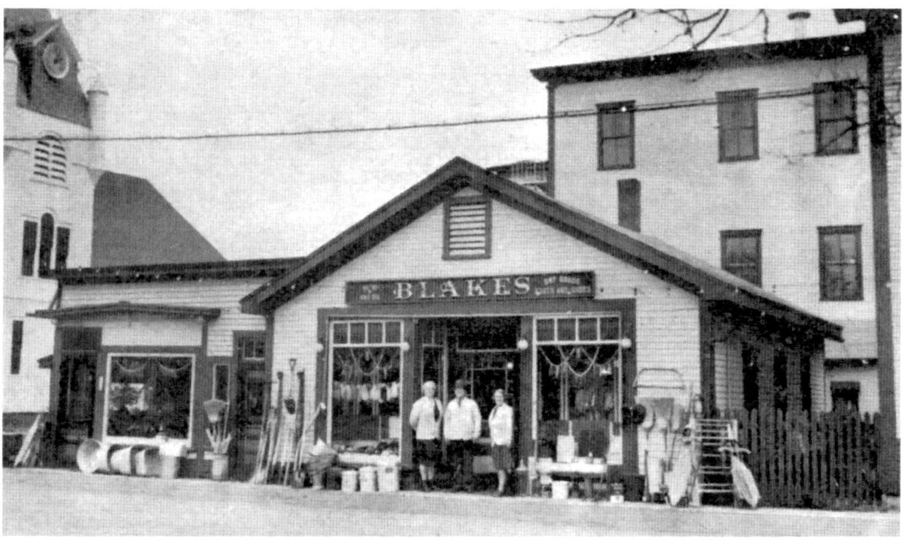

Blake's store, with diner in left area; Congregational Church (far left). *Courtesy of Joyce Wood's postcard collection.*

Bill Peaslee operated a little hot dog stand at the edge of the Common on summer nights, just opposite Candyland, facing Main Street. Later, it was taken over by Bob Cammett. And back in the late 1930s, my parents operated a fried clam stand on the same spot, catering to moviegoers at the Odd Fellows Hall on Friday nights.

Day's Potato Chips was not a restaurant, but it was a stop for folks on their way to the beach from Derry and towns south and west. This little potato chip factory was owned by Leonard and Marjorie Day. They sold chips, sodas and ice cream from a counter in the front part of the building. The factory consisted of a potato peeler, a slicer, a washtub, two frying kettles and tables on which the chips were dried and salted. I left the tip of a finger in the potato slicer and ruined a batch of potatoes.

The building was located just to the right of the eastbound onramp to Route 101. This was when Freetown Road was a little used connector from Chester and Fremont Roads to Route 101, now Route 27.

The Lazy C was a little pizza restaurant on the corner of Fremont Road and Paradise Drive, operating in the 1950s.

In 1978, the Silver Fox opened in a new building across from the Raymond Shopping Center. This was operated by Dominic and Dorothy Renda. Dominic was a talented chef, and the meals there were excellent. A fire put the Fox out of business in the late '80s, and the building was later razed.

The Pines restaurant is a favorite for seafood. It began as a little ice cream stand run by Arthur Shugrue. He lived on Long Hill Road on a parcel of land that extended down to what is now Route 27, then 101. He subdivided the restaurant lot from the remainder of the land. Doris Beachard may have operated it at one time. The restaurant is now owned by Norman Launier of Deerfield.

Directly across from the Pines, in the 1950s, Bessie's Lunch was located on the site of the former Griffin's Mill, operated by Merton and Bessie Healey. Later, they moved to Fremont and are now located on Route 125 in Brentwood.

Some folks will remember another ice cream stand, Penniwit, which was located in the area of the Branch Apartments. It offered jobs to many Raymond High School kids, and it was a very busy place on summer evenings.

Then there was Mr. Custard, a soft ice cream store in the building now housing a beauty shop and a used car and repair business. Mr. Custard was charged with allegedly setting fire to the building when business was slow.

Finally, I must mention McDonald's, arriving in 1979. Jack Barnes, profiled later in this book, had been an executive at McDonald's in Albany, New York. He had traveled through Raymond while attending the University of New Hampshire, stopped at Day's Potato Chips, and contrary to corporate advice, opined that Raymond would be a good location for a store. Good call.

Most of these businesses were located on what is now Route 27. Then, it was Route 101, the main route from Manchester and western New Hampshire to the seacoast.

Prior to 1939, the highway went through Raymond village, with a left turn at the Common. When the "cement road" was built in the late '30s, it bypassed the village but continued through the business districts of Epping, Exeter and Hampton.

Progress and Growth: Good or Bad?

Census year	population
1960	1,867
1970	3,003
1980	5,453
1990	8,854
2000	9,697
2010	10,138

Growth does not come without problems: increased traffic, higher taxes for more schools, perhaps less sense of community.

As of this writing, there are five traffic lights in Raymond. There were none in 1960. Most are the result of the change to Freetown Road and the completion of Route 101. Yes, they are some inconvenience to those of us who remember the no-traffic-light era. But certainly, for someone from Manchester or Boston, it must seem like country.

New blood has added vitality to the old town's veins. Many of the newer residents are very interested in the town's affairs, and they volunteer on committees and boards.

It must be acknowledged that sometimes a relatively new resident is resented for his or her efforts or ideas. To an old-time resident, the thought of making Raymond into a carbon copy of a Massachusetts suburb is anathema. Yet many newer residents appreciate Raymond's country flavor and are happy to preserve it. "Preservation" does not go unchallenged, though. Some see such efforts as an attack on individual property rights.

One can imagine a native farmer's annoyance of newly settled neighbors' opposition to the farmer's subdivision on the grounds that the loss of the pastoral view will devalue their homes. Implicit is that the farmer should maintain the view for the benefit of the neighbors.

So without going into the politics of the issue, it can be said that there are reasonable arguments for and against various factors involved in growth.

The first growth spurt in modern times came about in the mid-1960s, when the Green Hills subdivision was created. This was a mobile home park in which lots were owned rather than rented.

Another development from the 1970s was known as Fordway Brook. Located on Lane Road, the tract was purchased from a Hazen Wyman who had a sawmill on the site. An entrepreneur from New York by the name of Richard Beck subdivided the parcel and built moderately priced Cape Cod–style homes and ranches. They sold very well, and this was a cause of the population increase in that decade.

Since then, new streets and subdivisions have been added here and there. Green Road, which was unpaved in the 1950s and had not a single house from the Dodge-Heath cemetery to Scribner Road, is now suburbia.

4

CHURCHES

Raymond Baptist Church

By Janice Hedman

The Raymond Baptist Church found its humble beginnings as the Raymond Community Bible Club. Its first pastor was Ivor Sellevoog. In the spring of 1950, the group began making plans to be incorporated as the Evangelical Community Church of Raymond, which was later finalized under the leadership of new pastor Robert Draper. With great enthusiasm, the church's first Sunday school program was started in September 1950. During this time, the present annex building was purchased and served as the church meeting place for many years. The church looks to February 12, 1951, as the date of its official beginnings.

John Johnson came to serve as pastor of this young congregation from 1951 to 1954. Later, Jack Cavanaugh was called to be pastor, serving until 1957. Through the influence of Reverend Cavanaugh and Gerald Bradley, who followed him, the church became affiliated with the Conservative Baptist Association and changed its name to Raymond Baptist Church.

In September 1962, Richard Johnson began his nineteen years of service as pastor. In 1964, land was purchased for the construction of a church building. In 1965, the foundation was poured, capped and used for worship services. In 1967, the sanctuary was completed. Reverend Johnson served

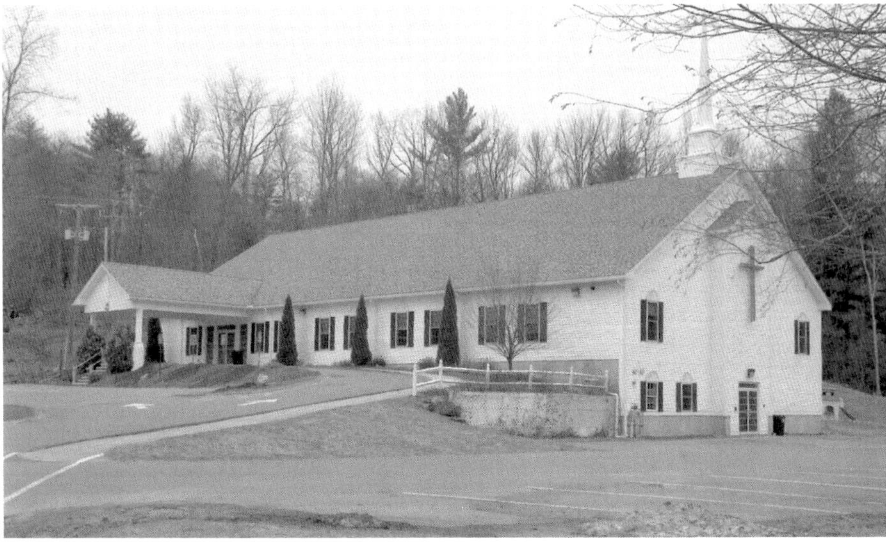

The present building of Raymond Baptist Church. *Courtesy of Paul Brown.*

until September 1981. Reverend Roy Glave came to serve as pastor in 1982 until March 1986. In 1984, Mike Chouinard was hired on a part-time basis as associate pastor. In March 1986, Reverend Glave faced serious health concerns and retired. Mike then served as interim pastor until January 1987, at which time he was voted to be the pastor. He was ordained in 1992.

On August 31, 2003, after seventeen years as pastor, Mike Chouinard gave his last sermon and retired from the ministry to take a position in the Raymond school system, as he felt that God was leading him to work with the youth in the community. Mike remains an active member of our church family, heading the youth group and participating in several other ministries.

Following Mike Chouinard's retirement as pastor, our church was blessed to have one of our deacons, Reverend Kent Threlfall, serve as interim pastor from 2003 to 2005. Kent enabled the church to transition from a longtime pastorate and prepare for a new chapter in its life.

In March 2004, we moved into our new church building on the RBC campus. All three buildings are used for various meeting rooms, Sunday school classes, youth group meetings and functions. The new building comfortably seats three hundred attendees with the ability to remove temporary walls to expand to five hundred when the time comes.

In October 2005, we welcomed Dr. Reverend Kevin McBride as our new pastor. Pastor McBride graduated from Boston University with a major in aerospace engineering, and was an aerospace engineer before entering the ministry after graduating from Gordon Conwell Theological Seminary. He grew up in New York and then moved to Boston, where he met his wife, Diane. He was senior associate pastor at First Baptist Church in Portland, Maine, prior to coming to RBC and has been in the pastorate for over twenty-five years.

As we celebrate over fifty years as a church, we rejoice at the changes in the church and surrounding community and continue to look for ways to reach out to the community. We sponsor several missionaries throughout the world as well as provide Bible study and outreach programs for people in the local area.

Bethany Church

By Mark Grant

Bethany Church, at 90 Chester Road in Raymond, has been in existence since May 2011. However, its history dates back to 1990, when it opened its doors as Fellowship in Christ under the direction of Pastor Harold Small. In September 2002, William Mahoney became the church's pastor and served for several years while the church was under the name Eaglebrook Church. In 2008, the church offered its property to Bethany Church in Greenland.

Bethany Church's history dates back to the 1800s and, with the recent adoption of Eaglebrook Church, created a new platform of ministry that would build on a strong biblical teaching and local engagement in community service projects through its outreach and caring programs. In May 2011, under the leadership of Pastor Mark Rivera, Bethany Church's Raymond Campus launched New Hampshire's first multisite church.

Bethany Church offers scriptural preaching and teaching in a contemporary format while embracing a strong commitment to Christian discipleship, family and community. Its mission statement is "To be a Christian community where the love of God is transforming us from the Inside Out and our love for God is drawing the Outside In."

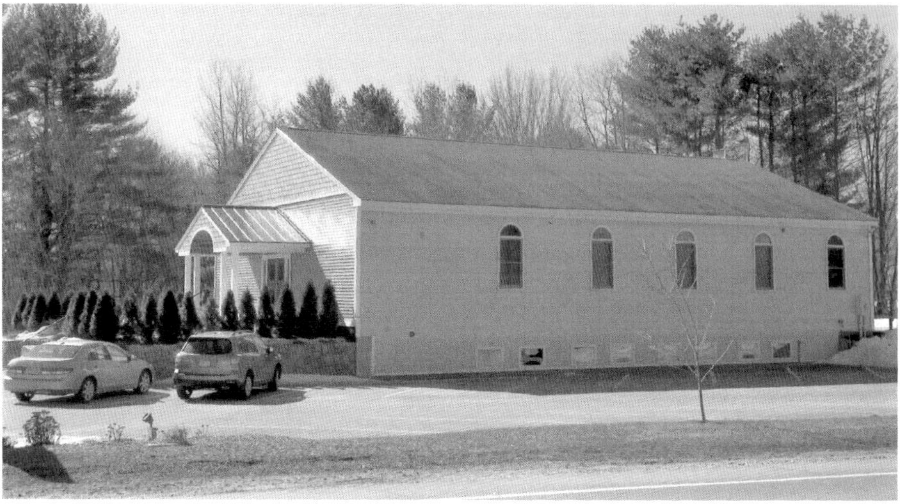

Bethany Church on Chester Road. *Courtesy of Paul Brown.*

Sunday worship services are held at 9:00 and 11:00 a.m. with children and student programs at both. Midweek programs on Wednesday evenings are also offered.

St. Joseph Parish

By Tom Carleton

In 1987, the St. Raymond Mission Church and St. Joseph of Epping were brought together and a new church was constructed and dedicated on Route 27 in Epping. The St. Raymond Church was sold in 1990. St. Joseph Parish is where the St. Raymond Chapel now resides and is also the location for the original stained-glass window donated by Richard Ladd of Raymond.

In 2010, as St. Joseph celebrated the twentieth anniversary of the current parish building and the consolidation of St. Raymond and St. Joseph Churches, there was need for additional space. The parish had limited space for meetings, teaching, activities and storage and lacked an office. The addition of a Perpetual Adoration Chapel would provide the opportunity for silent and private prayer.

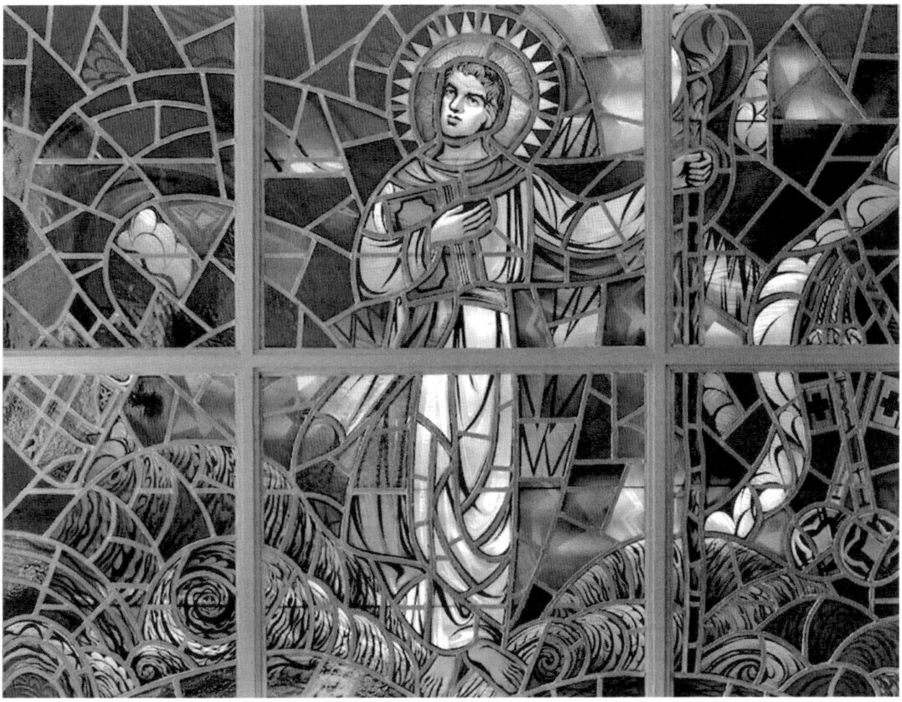

Stained-glass window in St. Joseph's Church from St. Raymond's Church. *Courtesy of Tom Carleton.*

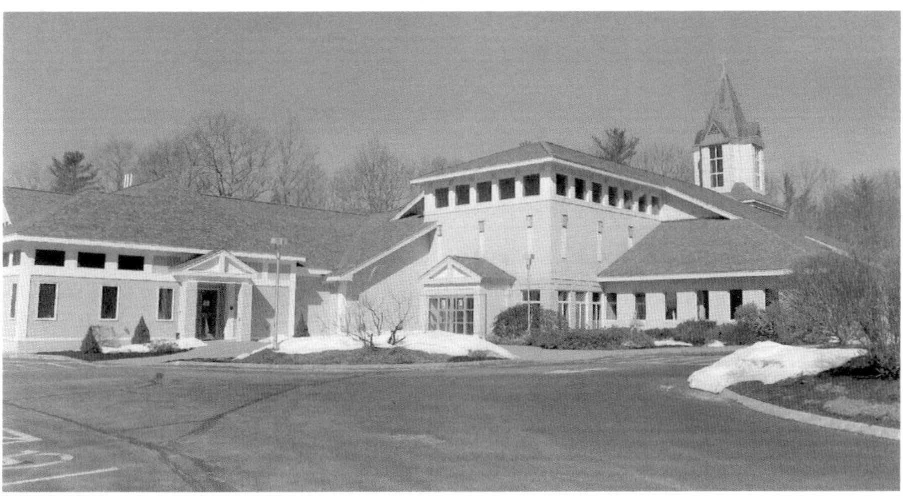

St. Joseph's Church. *Courtesy of Paul Brown.*

In the fall of 2010, the parish formulated a plan to support future needs by conducting a pledge fundraising plan similar to the process that built the church more than twenty years before. The successful pledge drive and Diocese of Manchester support allowed the parish to move forward with the building plan. Ground breaking took place in April 2011, and the addition was started in June 2011 and completed in May 2012. The new rectory was also built, and the old rectory, located on Church Street in Epping, was sold.

The new facilities were dedicated by the Most Reverend Peter Anthony Libasci, the tenth bishop of Manchester, on March 10, 2012.

Pastors of St. Joseph Parish, Epping New Hampshire

Reverend Joseph E. Vaccarest	1940–1947
Reverend Rodolphe L. Drapeau	1947–1948
Reverend Victor A. Dagenais	1948–1956
Reverend Armand J. Provost	1956–1966
Reverend Louis A. Langevin	1966–1976
Reverend Leo L. Frechette	1976–1985
Reverend Ronald E. Corriveau	1985–2002
Reverend Michael S. Taylor	2002–2008
Reverend Volney J. DeRosia	2008–2013
Reverend Donald E. Clinton	2013–present

The Congregational Church of Raymond

By Kathryn Fongeallaz

In 1976, the year of our nation's bicentennial, the church was decorated with bunting for the week of festivities, the Ladies Benevolent Society sold its cookbook *Meeting House Recipes*, commemorative plates and tiles were offered and the choir presented the first "Bean Tavern." Dinner was prepared and served while music and entertainment were presented by the choir in the tavern style of 1776. The church year began with the announcement of a $15,000 gift from Linda and Carlton Fisk toward the new two-level addition of classrooms, offices and an all-purpose room. Work on this addition continued until its dedication on May 27, 1979.

In February 1978, Reverend Neil Iverson became pastor, a position he would hold for the next twenty-six years.

The Raymond Congregational Church celebrated its 150th anniversary on May 27, 1984. For this occasion, the life of the church from its beginning in 1834 through 1984 was chronicled by church member Iber Holmes Gove. The steeple clocks (often referred to as the "town" clocks) were upgraded with electricity, and the carillons were installed. A special meeting of the church authorized the residing of the church building, and with gifts from individuals, work was completed for the 150th anniversary celebration. The first Christmas Bean Tavern celebration was held.

The church experienced continued good fortune throughout the '80s, as evidenced by reports of church committees. At the end of the decade, $15,000 had been raised to restore the sanctuary and refinish the organ. Volunteers logged over six hundred hours of hard work to restore and refinish the original pews at minimal cost.

In 1989, the family of Dorothy Blake Tilton established a substantial endowment in her memory, and the interest was to be used to provide an uplifting cultural or arts program each year. Dorothy was a descendant of the Blake family, who donated the land to the Congregational Society for its church and former parsonage in 1834 and also gave the land to the Town of Raymond for its Common.

The years preceding Reverend Iverson's retirement in September 2004 were productive, with the congregation growing and the church prospering. Due to strong lay leadership, the church was able to weather the changes after his retirement and throughout the search for an interim pastor, who was installed in January 2005. Reverend Charles Redfern led the church until November 2006, when a permanent pastor, Reverend Richard Robinson, was called. Membership faltered as traditions and visions for the future were not compatible. Financial concerns led to questions of the viability of retaining a full-time pastor, and during this discussion, Reverend Robinson resigned to seek other opportunities.

Again, strong lay leadership maintained weekly worship and other activities of the church. In March 2009, Reverend Ginny Slawnwhite became supply pastor until a permanent pastor was appointed. After months of work, the deacons, trustees and search committee agreed that the church could no longer afford a full-time pastor. They considered several applicants and finally called Reverend Slawnwhite to be permanent pastor in September 2011.

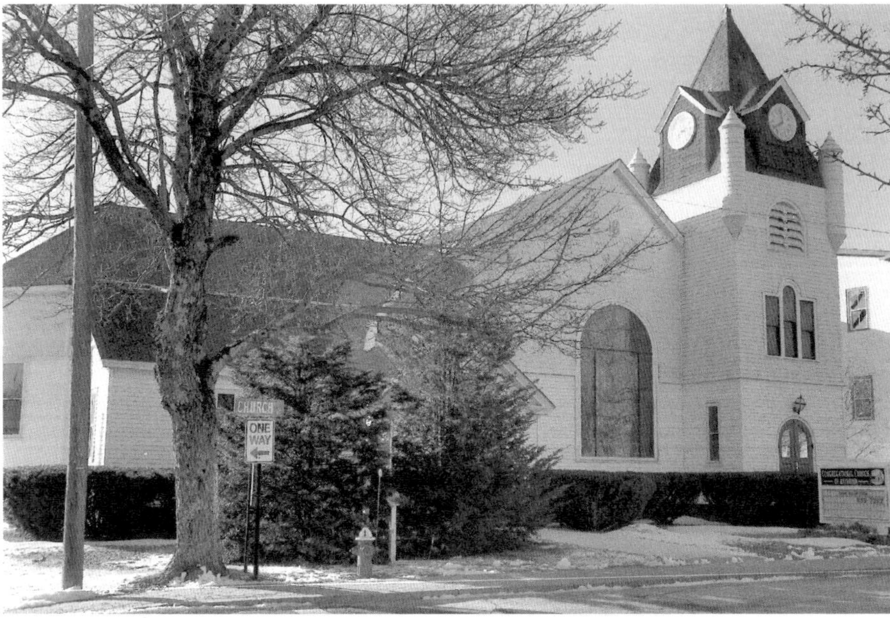

Raymond Congregational Church. *Courtesy of Paul Brown.*

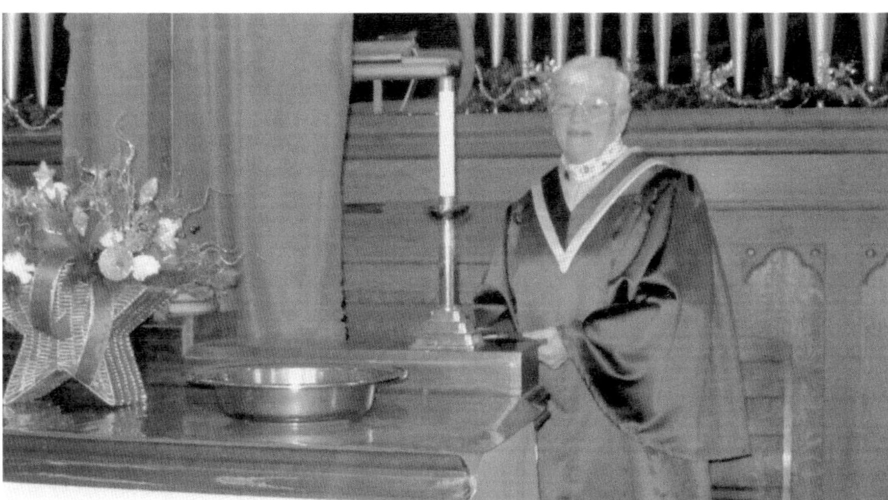

Geneva Clifford, organist and choir director at Raymond Congregational Church. *Courtesy of Sally Paradis.*

In 2007, the trustees appointed a "Steeple Committee" to oversee much-needed repairs to the historic church building. The needed amount of $50,000 was raised to allow for the replacement of siding on the upper part of the church's exterior, window repair and painting, foundation restoration, clock repair and new technology to operate the carillon. Work was completed in time for the 175th anniversary of the church, with a celebration and rededication service held October 17, 2009.

No church history would be complete without honoring the fifty-three years of dedicated service of organist and choir director Geneva Clifford. She has led the music ministry through the terms of many pastors, changing leadership, fluctuating membership and financial hardships and has done it all with grace and enthusiasm.

History of the Methodist Church in Raymond

By Gayle McMullen

There have been Methodists in Raymond since 1825. The current church has been located on the corners of Wight and Main Streets since 1894.

For brief periods in 1956–1958, 1963 and 1970, the Congregational and Methodist Churches tried various methods of combining the congregations through yoking or alternating churches during the summer months. Three members from each church were elected to serve on the Inter-Church Council when they were yoked. Pastors serving included Reverend Douglas Moore and W.E. Mack in the 1950s and Reverend Alton Mark in 1970.

In 1977, the Reed family commissioned Raymond resident Russell Ege to craft a stained-glass window in memory of Orrin C. Reed. This was installed at the front of the sanctuary above the organ. Repairs were made to the wood frame around the window by the Reed family in 2010.

The matching round stained-glass window at the back of the sanctuary was also made by Mr. Ege. It was crafted in honor of Cyrus and Georgina Smith at the request of the Smith family and was dedicated before their deaths in 1979 and 1987, respectively.

In the 1980s and '90s, changes were made in the form of vinyl siding, a ramp to Fellowship Hall and repairs to the steeple. At this time, the weather vane that had topped the steeple was removed. In 2004, the steeple was

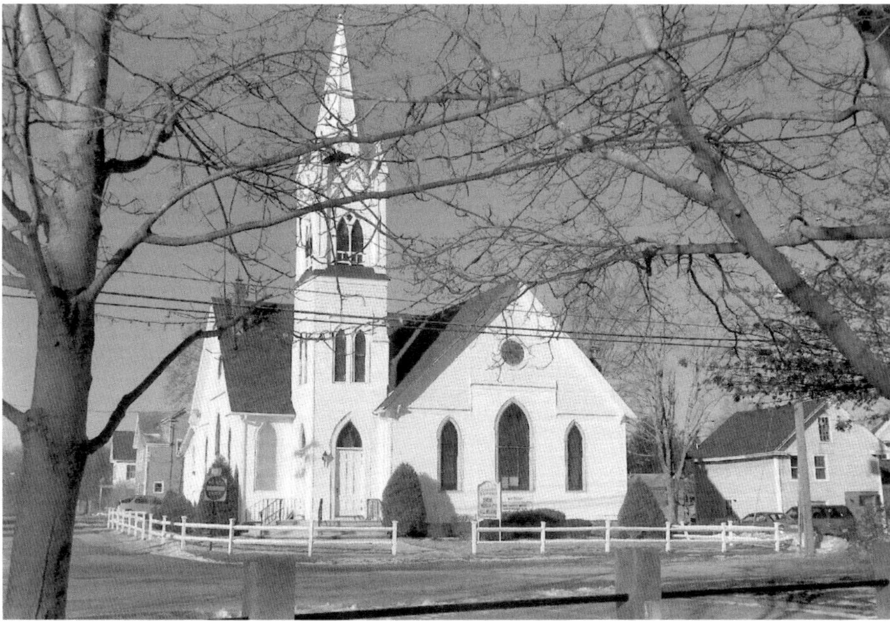

The Methodist Church. *Courtesy of Paul Brown.*

struck by lightning. Lightning rods have since been placed on the church roof and fellowship hall, and a fire alarm system installed. Cosmetic changes include landscaping, fencing and a new sign. Repairs to the three front stained-glass windows were made possible with a donation in memory of Dr. George H. Guptill.

Pastors who have served the church since 1977 are Richard Moore, Bruce Angus, Charles Kern, Anthony Jarek-Glidden, David Whitford, Kwan Y. Lee, Jan Parke, Neal P. White and Carroll Moore.

The Village Kindergarten has rented rooms downstairs for many years. An AA group meets in the fellowship hall weekly. Since 2004, the church has shared a pastor with North Salem UMC. The United Methodist Women meet monthly and actively assist needy organizations.

New Life Assembly of God

By Brian Tranes

The history of New Life Assembly of God starts with a man named Charles Holt, supported by the sister church of Trinity Assembly of God in Derry, New Hampshire, and his desire to start an Assemblies of God church in Raymond. New Life Church is a biblically centered church that accompanies people on their personal faith journey with God.

The first church service was held on August 3, 1980, in the Raymond Lions Club with a handful of people. A few months later New Life Church was averaging fifty-seven people in attendance. Over the next two years, the church would continue to grow and flourish.

By 1984, the congregation had grown to an attendance of between eighty and one hundred people and quickly became too big to continue meeting in the Lions Club. As the church awaited the completion of its permanent seven-thousand-square-foot home on Route 156 in Raymond, the congregation met in a variety of places, including the Walnut Hill Seminar House, Lamprey River Elementary School and the Raymond Junior-Senior High School. The congregation began services in the bottom floor of its new building in the spring of 1985, as members awaited the completion of the main level.

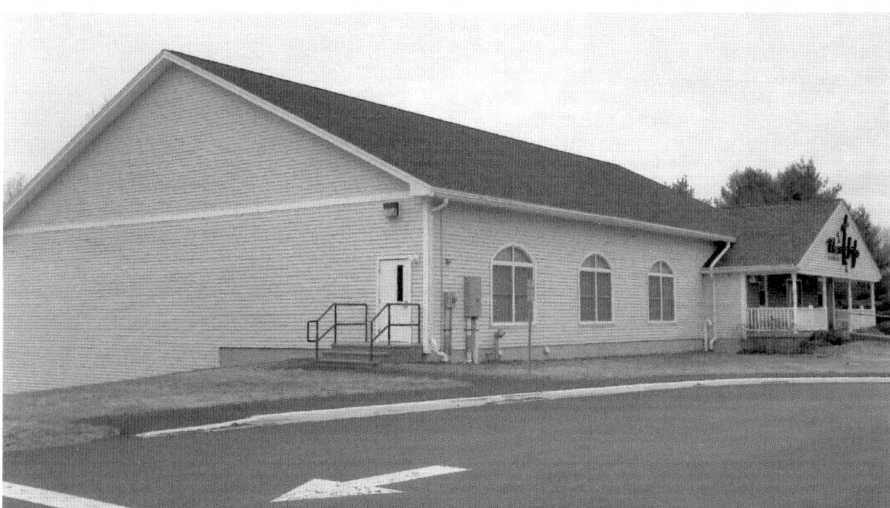

New Life Assembly of God's present building. *Courtesy of Paul Brown.*

In the fall of 1985, New Life Church opened Sonshine Preschool and Daycare with an enrollment of forty-five children. Over the next five years, Sonshine continued to offer its services to the community of Raymond and the surrounding towns.

In 1987, New Life accepted their second senior pastor, Moses Baker, who led New Life church for a few years.

Their current pastor, Ken Bosse, began pastoring New Life Church in 1991, with a core group of 65 hardworking and fun-loving people. The church quickly grew from 65 to 240 by maintaining a loving atmosphere of acceptance. Due to continued growth, New Life expanded its facilities in 2008 to more than double its current size, with the potential for further expansion. Its mission statement is "Welcoming People to Experience New Life in Jesus Christ."

New Life is a contemporary church with lively music and life application messages. It offers a variety of children's and youth programs. Coffee and refreshments between the two Sunday morning services is a great time for people to connect.

Church and State

By Paul Brown

*Raymond: "Worldly men who love money better than God"**

In this enlightened age, we are extremely careful about mixing government with religion. The American Civil Liberties Union has sued public school systems for offering prayer. The "ten commandments" (note that I did not capitalize the two words in the quotes) have been banned from certain courthouses. Indeed, the wall of separation between church and state is quite high and thick.

**The Exeter, New Market and South New Market Directory and History, 1872.*

It was not always thus. When I was a kid in public school, we were required to repeat the Lord's Prayer as part of our "morning exercises," which included a pledge of allegiance to the flag, the words "under God" being added during my school years.

In short, within human memory, religion, primarily Christian, was accepted without question as part of public education and endorsed by the state.

And up until 1819, the church was the government in Raymond and the rest of New England. And that church was the Congregational Church.

In 1641, New Hampshire, which had been a separate province since the first settlements in 1623, came under the authority of Massachusetts. This was unappreciated by many settlers who were here for business and not religious purposes, and the enmity that was created has not been fully erased in over four centuries.

In 1649, Charles I, king of England and America, made a serious mistake when dealing with the Puritans in England. His head was separated from his body in one of those scenes the English were famous for in those days. This may be where the term "head of state" originated.

In any case, the Puritans solidified their power in New Hampshire. During that time, church attendance was mandatory. The tithingmen and constables enforced the law that

> *all and every person and persons whatever shall, on the Lord's day, carefully apply themselves to duties of religion and piety publicly and privately, and no tradesman, artificer, laborer, or other person whatever shall upon the land or otherwise do or exercise any labor, business, or work of their ordinary callings, not engage in any games, sport, play or recreation on the Lord's day, or any part there of (works of necessity and charity only excepted) upon penalty that every person so offending shall forfeit five shillings.*

Quakers were severely treated. If returning to town after banishment, the punishment was removal of an ear. The other ear followed with a second offense.

More offenses brought burning a hole through the tongue with a hot poker, and so on. Ultimately, death would end any further transgressions, such as continuing to be a Quaker.

It can only be imagined that some of the settlers in New Hampshire, accustomed as they were in going about the business of fishing, trading, trapping, logging and hunting, would find such interference intolerable.

Yet, the church, becoming known as "Congregational," was the government and the law. Taxes were levied by the church and paid to the church for the building and upkeep of the meetinghouses and payment for the ministers.

During this time, in all likelihood, the wilderness to the west of Exeter, which included what we know as Raymond, was inhabited by trappers, woodsmen and hunters, as well as a few remaining Indians. Whoever was here probably didn't give a fig about the church's rules.

In 1658, Oliver Cromwell, the "Great Protector," died, and the next year, King Charles II regained the throne, probably to the relief of the non-Puritans in England.

Certainly it was a relief to the New Hampshire settlers, although Massachusetts continued in its rigid church doctrine, culminating in the witch trials of the 1690s. Interestingly, some witches were pardoned by the Massachusetts legislature in 1957; the remainder* were not until quite recently in 2001. So much for Massachusetts's liberalism.

In New Hampshire, the church was still the government, and it continued to be until well after the Revolution.

In Raymond, after incorporation, the attitude was likely a continuation of the outlaw spirit that had guided the early settlers. There were disagreements as to where the church/meetinghouse should be located. Probably a goodly number preferred the tavern at Bean's, while others wanted a more formal environment away from the rum. In spite of these differences, it appears that there was toleration for non-Congregationalists who were exempted from paying the minister's salary. It seems that Mr. Bean was paid for feeding the minister, but that was probably accepted because he was also paid to provide rum at the meetings.

Disagreements over religion were set aside during the Revolution, when people had to choose sides: either with the Loyalists, or with the rebels. Raymond, being recently Freetown, where trees were not given up to the king, was probably rebel in its leanings.

And once the British were defeated and the work of establishing a new country was commenced, the rules had to be considered.

New Hampshire already had a constitution that considered the rights of individuals over the state. As the various states debated over wording, freedom from a state religion emerged as a right that all could agree on.

---

*One of the more recently pardoned was Margaret Scott, one of my ancestors, some eleven generations ago.

So as early as 1803, twelve years after the first amendment was ratified, John Muzzy of Amherst brought action against the local assessors. He had been jailed because he refused to pay seventy-five cents toward the Congregational minister's salary. The judge, who apparently heeded the law of the land, decided in favor of Muzzy, a Presbyterian.

Over the next few years, it soon became obvious that the constitution said what it said, and in 1819, the Toleration Act was passed, finally ending Congregationalism's hold on New Hampshire government.

5

HISTORY OF THE DUDLEY-TUCKER LIBRARY

BY LINDA HOELZEL

The Dudley-Tucker Library opened its doors in September 1908. On March 13, 1917, after town meeting, the town hall burned down. From then until the new town hall was built in 1974, the selectmen's offices were located on the second floor of the library. By the mid-1980s, the library's ability to meet the ever-increasing needs of the community was hampered greatly by lack of space. The library was renovated in 1994 with an addition to add much-needed space and to make the entire library handicap accessible. During the renovation, the library conducted business as usual in temporary quarters in the old fire station.

On May 23, 1994, the trustees and staff welcomed the community to the dedication and open house in the enlarged and renovated library. Before the expansion/renovation, the entire library was housed on the main floor of the library. The second floor would not hold the weight of shelving and books, and the basement was not usable. The renovation allowed the library to use the second floor for adult and young adult titles and office space. The Children's Room now occupies the basement of the building. The larger Children's Room now allows children to have their own space for story time and special programming. In 1990, the library participated in the first statewide summer reading program. Since then, participation in the summer reading program has increased each year.

In March 1978, the first Friends of the Library group was formed with around twenty members. The current Friends of the Library was formed in 1997. The Friends of the Dudley-Tucker Library is a 501(c)(3) nonprofit organization that helps the library provide programs, services and materials not covered by the library's normal operating budget. Its two main fundraisers each year are an annual book sale in July and an annual holiday raffle in December.

Throughout the years, the library has had a number of dedicated trustees. Three library trustees held the position for a number of years. Iber Holmes Gove was a trustee from 1964 until 1994. Ruth Brooks Hoffman was a descendant of one of the original founders of the library and held the position of library trustee from 1972 until 1984. In 1984, her daughter, Barbara Hoffman Beardsley, was elected and served as a trustee until 2013.

The library's first computer was installed in 1986 and was used to update patron files and catalogue new materials. In 1991, the library installed an automated circulation system. Our newest circulation system includes a card catalogue that allows patrons to renew items from home, request a new title or an inter-library loan online or write a book review on our card catalogue.

The library is ever evolving. Looking into the future, the library will continue to adapt to new technologies while supporting traditional modes of information.

Dudley-Tucker Librarians

Lewis O. Pollard, 1908
Charles Poor, 1908–1909 (shared)
Jessie Prescott, 1908–1909 (shared)
Edith Bartlett Tilton, 1909–1926
Alice Littlefield Wason, 1926–1973
Marjorie von Suck, 1973–1977
Linda Sordillo, 1977–1978
Janet Brown, 1978–1986
Sherry Brox, 1986–2011
Linda Hoelzel, 2011–present

The Tucker Family

By Paul Brown

Gilman Henry Tucker, a Raymond native, was descended from three prominent families: the Tuckers, Dudleys and Gilmans. He was grandson of one of the earliest settlers and son of Henry Tucker, a general in the New Hampshire militia.

Tucker attended Dartmouth and found his fortune in Boston and New York. He became well connected in New York City society; Andrew Carnegie was among his friends. His friendship with Carnegie secured the grant that established and built the Dudley-Tucker Library.

Tucker never forgot his hometown. He maintained the home where he was raised on Long Hill, enlarged it, and some of the property has remained with his stepdescendants. The dwelling was known as the Browsing, and it was a home of exceptional quality. Unfortunately, it was destroyed by fire in the 1960s. A "mounting stone," a three-step granite block used to assist ladies into carriages, still exists. It has "The Browsing" and dates of the purchase and rebuildings chiseled on its sides.

Tucker was known as an orator and spoke at homecomings, describing the Raymond of his childhood. He is buried in the family cemetery off Long Hill Road.

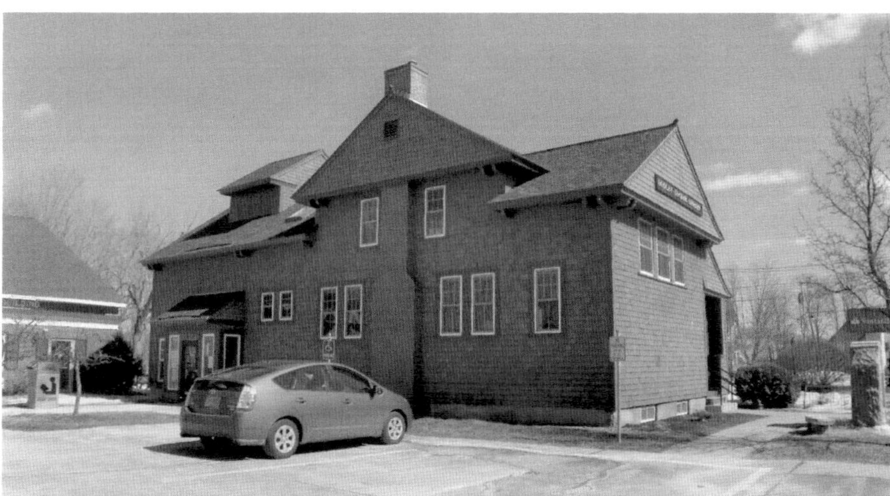

Dudley-Tucker Library, showing its newer addition. *Courtesy of Paul Brown.*

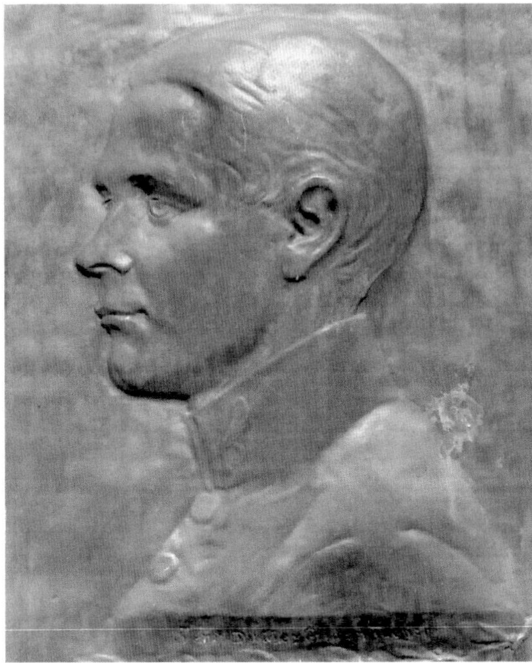

Plaque at Dudley-Tucker Library memorial to World War I soldiers, with likeness of Dudley Tucker. *Courtesy of Paul Brown.*

Tucker's son, Dudley Gilman Tucker, should be mentioned. He was raised in New York but enjoyed summers in Raymond. He graduated from Harvard in 1907 and joined his father in the textbook publishing business.

As World War I was beginning in Europe, but before the United States became involved, Dudley Tucker joined the French Foreign Legion to fight the Germans in France. Soon he became a member of the Lafayette Escadrille and received his pilot's wings.

He was shot down and killed, it is said, being chased by six German planes.

After the war, his mother went to France, disinterred his body and reinterred it at Versailles, France, in a memorial to the Escadrille.

A 1958 movie, *Lafayette Escadrille*, in which Clint Eastwood has one of his early roles, features Dudley Tucker briefly as one of the characters.

6

SCHOOLS

BY KATHLEEN HOELZEL AND SANDRA ELLIS

After the building of the Consolidated School in 1917, four small additions were constructed, the last being four classrooms in 1948. When voters passed a $148,000 bond issue in 1959 to construct the new 200 wing to house its high school students, it was referred to as a "giant step," and just five years later, the 300 wing, named for thirty-six-year elementary teacher Ruth T. Houghton, was added, with eight additional classrooms, a library and a kitchen/cafeteria.

The '60s ushered in population growth not experienced before in southeastern New Hampshire, giving rise to new cooperative school districts being formed and many being studied. Raymond joined the Pawtuckaway Study with Epping and Candia; however, the plan was defeated in 1969.

By the early '70s, the Raymond Consolidated School was bursting at the seams. Chairman of the school board Frank Case wrote in his report to the citizens in 1971: "If there was one word that may describe the major problem that besets every school district in southeast New Hampshire, it is GROWTH!"

In the '60s, Raymond's school enrollment had increased from 503 to over 900 students. With no positive action on a cooperative arrangement and defeat of two bond issues, the school board petitioned the state Department of Education for permission to operate on "split sessions" in 1972–73, utilizing the existing building for nearly eleven hours a day. First through fourth grades and ninth through twelfth grades attended the shortened morning session, and fifth through eighth went to the afternoon session. Such arrangement would continue until June 1976. In the meantime, school enrollment had doubled from 630 in 1966 to 1,213 in 1976.

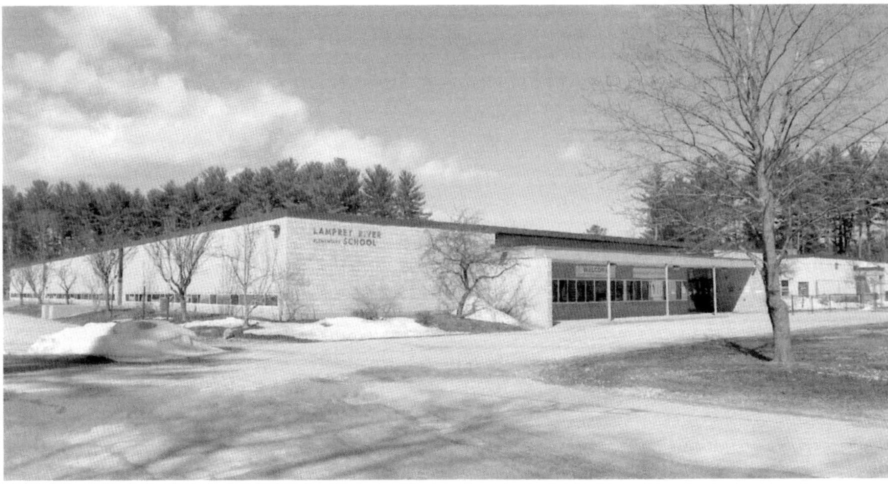

Lamprey River Elementary School. *Courtesy of Paul Brown.*

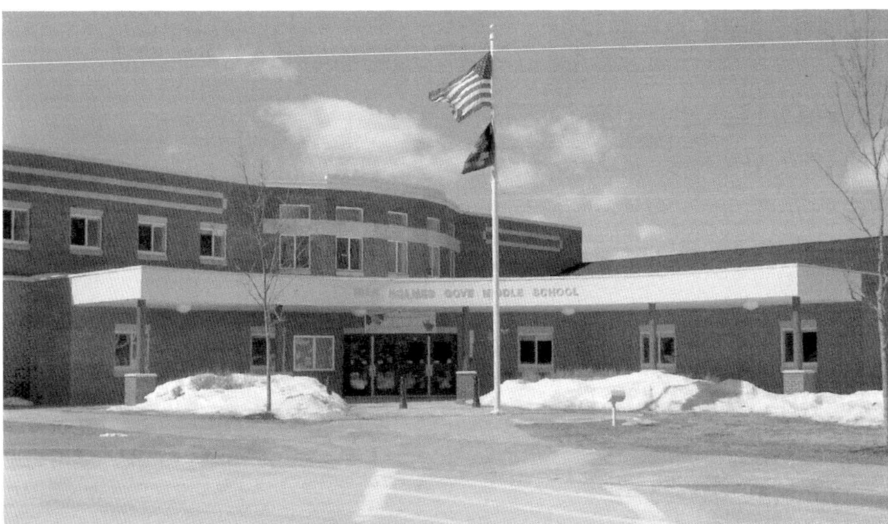

Iber Holmes Gove Middle School. *Courtesy of Paul Brown.*

The headline in the March 2, 1975 *New Hampshire Sunday News* reported "Raymond Votes $1.5 M School." The article continues, "It was the culmination of a lengthy controversy, but the end of Raymond's struggle over whether to spend $1.5 million to build a new school came quietly

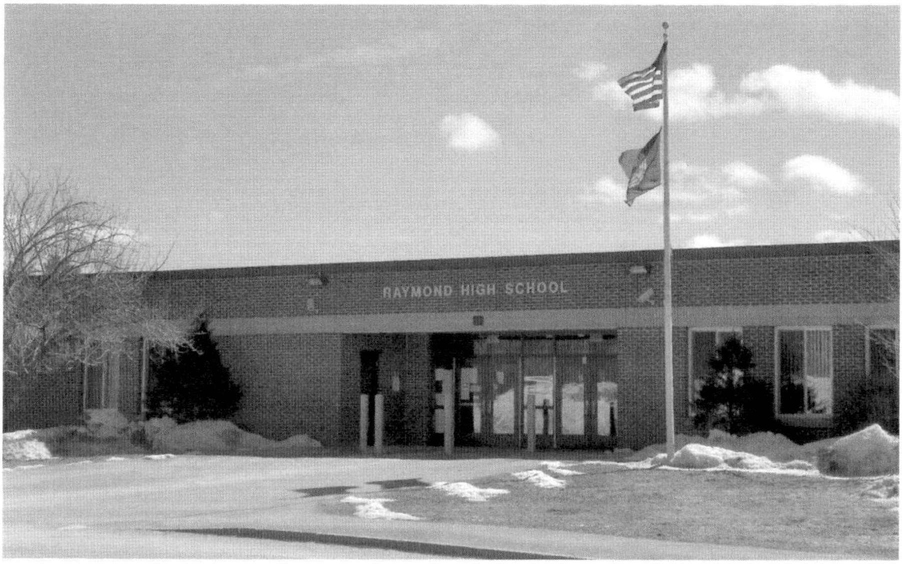

Raymond High School. *Courtesy of Paul Brown.*

tonight at a special school meeting. The town voted more than two to one in favor of building the school. The final vote was 600 to 294, with 901 of the town's 2,000 registered voters showing up for the special afternoon and evening meeting at the Raymond School gymnasium." The measure, needing a two-thirds vote, passed by a narrow margin of 6 votes.

The new six-hundred-pupil Lamprey River Elementary School (LRES) for grades one through six was constructed on seventeen acres along Old Manchester Road. The new community gymnasium was constructed at the seventh through twelfth grade school site off Epping Street, and the old gym was transformed into a media center. LRES was dedicated to the "Citizens of Raymond" and the community gymnasium to John J. Callaghan, long-serving high school principal, teacher and coach, on November 7, 1976.

Energy-saving renovations to the 100 wing were accomplished with federal funds. With Bureau of Outdoor Recreation funds, ball fields were improved, land was acquired behind the LRES for recreation and beach access, and a new soccer field was constructed with assistance from local businesses and residents offering in-kind contributions to be matched. These improvements were made possible by the inspiration, dedication and hard work of school board member Hughin Holt, and in June 1984, the Holt

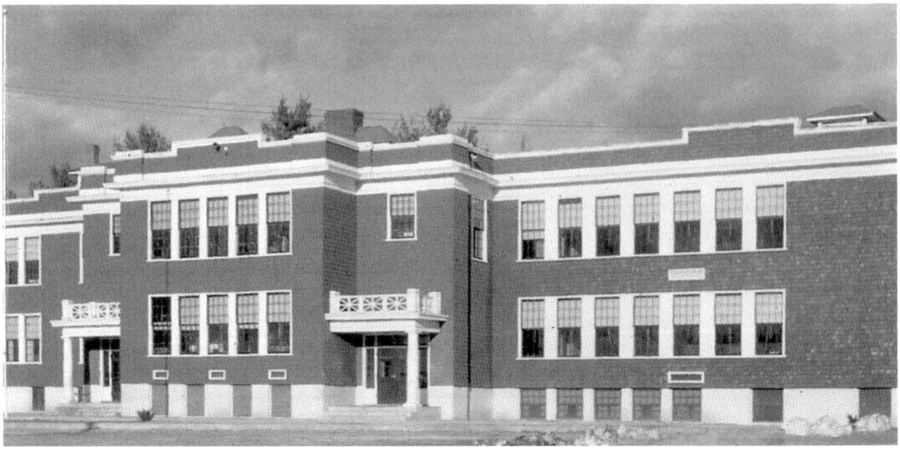

Raymond Consolidated School, which educated twelve grades in one building. *Courtesy of Paul Brown.*

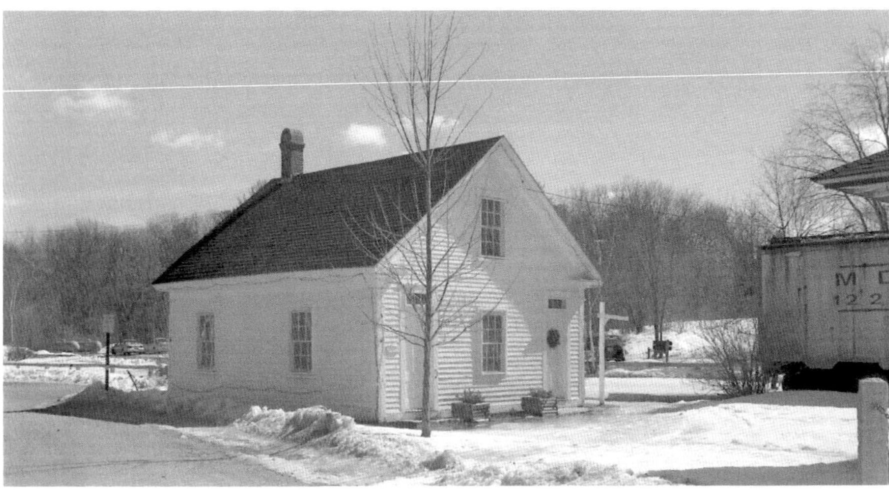

The Gile one-room schoolhouse is owned by the Raymond Historical Society. *Courtesy of Paul Brown.*

Field was dedicated to Hughin and family in recognition for "service to the Raymond School District."

During the '80s, an agreement was signed between the town and school district for the sharing of school facilities with town residents and organizations when not in use for school purposes.

Beginning in the fall of 1979, Raymond High School students were transported to the Exeter Vocational Center for a portion of their school day

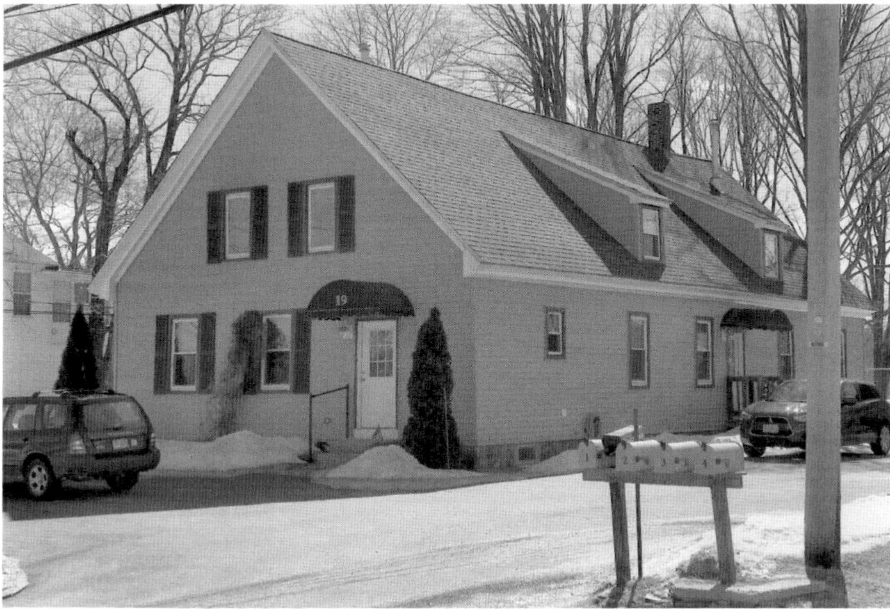

Pecker School, an early schoolhouse, now apartments. *Courtesy of Paul Brown.*

to attend technical and vocational programs offered at the Seacoast School of Technology. Presently, sixty-three students take advantage of this opportunity.

In 1984, the school board asked voters for approval to petition the state board of education to withdraw from the four-town School Administrative Unit #15 with Auburn, Candia and Hooksett to form its own SAU #33. The petition was overwhelmingly approved.

Voters approved a $6.6 million bond issue for the construction of a new high school in 1986, to be built on sixty-seven acres of land off Harriman Hill Road, opening in the fall of 1988. Before five years had lapsed, a Space Needs Committee was formed to consider alterations/additions to existing schools and a bond issue of $1.5 million for the construction of a two-hundred-pupil addition to the high school was approved in 1994.

The former junior-senior high school facility, renovated to house grades five through eight, was dedicated and renamed the Iber Holmes Gove Middle School (IHGMS) in honor of native daughter and former teacher Iber Holmes Gove "for her support and involvement in Raymond education."

In 1997, voters adopted official ballot voting (often referred to as "Senate Bill 2") that would change the way the annual, or "traditional," school district meeting would be held. The new legislation called for a first (deliberative)

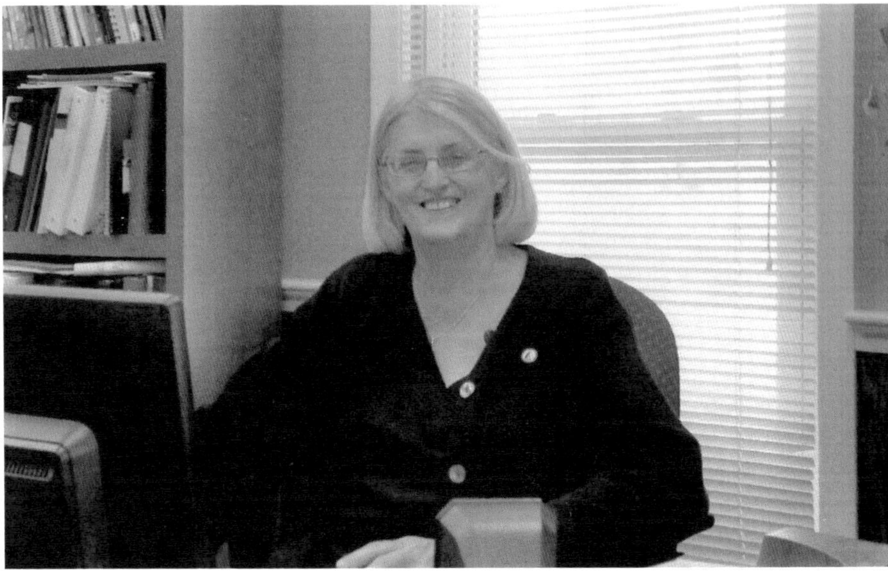

Ellen Small, school district administrator. *Courtesy of Paul Brown.*

session meeting, and a second (voting) session to be conducted on the day that town meeting elections are held.

In 2003, voters approved half-day kindergarten and a $985,000 bond issue for a five-classroom addition that carried a 75 percent reimbursement from the State of New Hampshire to be repaid over the life of the bond. (Raymond had been one of the last school districts in the state of New Hampshire to provide for public kindergarten.) That same year, LRES teacher Marilyn Benz Lindquist was named "New Hampshire Teacher of the Year."

Citizen groups joined forces and a proposal to build a new middle school on the footprint of the Raymond Consolidated School (razing the former building along with the 200 and 300 wings) was presented in 2005. The $13.8 million proposal was passed with 74 percent voter approval. The new IHGMS opened in the fall of 2006 and the connecting wing to the gym in January 2007. The IHGMS was named "Middle School of the Year in NH" in 2011. In 2012, principal Ellen Small was named "Middle School Principal of the Year in NH."

No stranger to the school district, Ellen Small, administrator in charge of superintendent services, began her forty-three-year career as a science teacher at the middle school in 1971 and served for several years as principal of IHGMS, prior to assuming her present role two years ago. Upon reflecting on events of the last four decades, she believes that the "defining moment" in the district was Raymond's vote to build a new high school in 1988, as it turned the tide from uncertainty about secondary education into a "commitment to educating its high school population" that continues today. Citing a moratorium at the state level on building aid until 2016, she sees no immediate solution to replacing the aging portable classrooms at LRES.

The Village Kindergarten

By Shirley Dodge (as reported to Paul Brown)

In 1958, Shirley Dodge started a kindergarten program for her own children that lasted for almost a half century. Starting with a small group of twelve students, the program moved from the Pilgrim Inn to the Congregational Parsonage and finally settled in the Methodist Church.

The need was really met with as many as fifty-five children with a pre-K class in morning and afternoon classes. There were six assistants during this time, "a real labor of love," says Mrs. Dodge.

The Raymond Village Kindergarten is still operating under the leadership of Diane Maddox.

7
CELEBRATIONS

National Bicentennial Celebration, July 1976

By Frank G. Case, Chairman

On July 19, 1975, the town received a letter indicating that the committee's plans for a celebration had been accepted and Raymond was officially designated as a National Bicentennial Community. A ceremony was held on August 22 on the town Common when the official bicentennial flag was presented to the town.

A commemorative coin designed by Ruth B. Hoffman, featuring the Bean Tavern and Raymond's original town hall was minted in silver, pewter and bronze at the W.H. Blackinton Company of Attleboro Falls, Massachusetts, in December. Bill Prince took on the job of distributing the coins for the Raymond Historical Society because of his interest as a collector. As one of its projects for the bicentennial year, the Raymond Historical Society prepared a highly acclaimed pictorial history published in May 1976 that is available for reviewing at the depot and town library.

The bicentennial dance, planned by Shirley Dodge and her committee, was held in the new Raymond Junior-Senior High School gymnasium. The

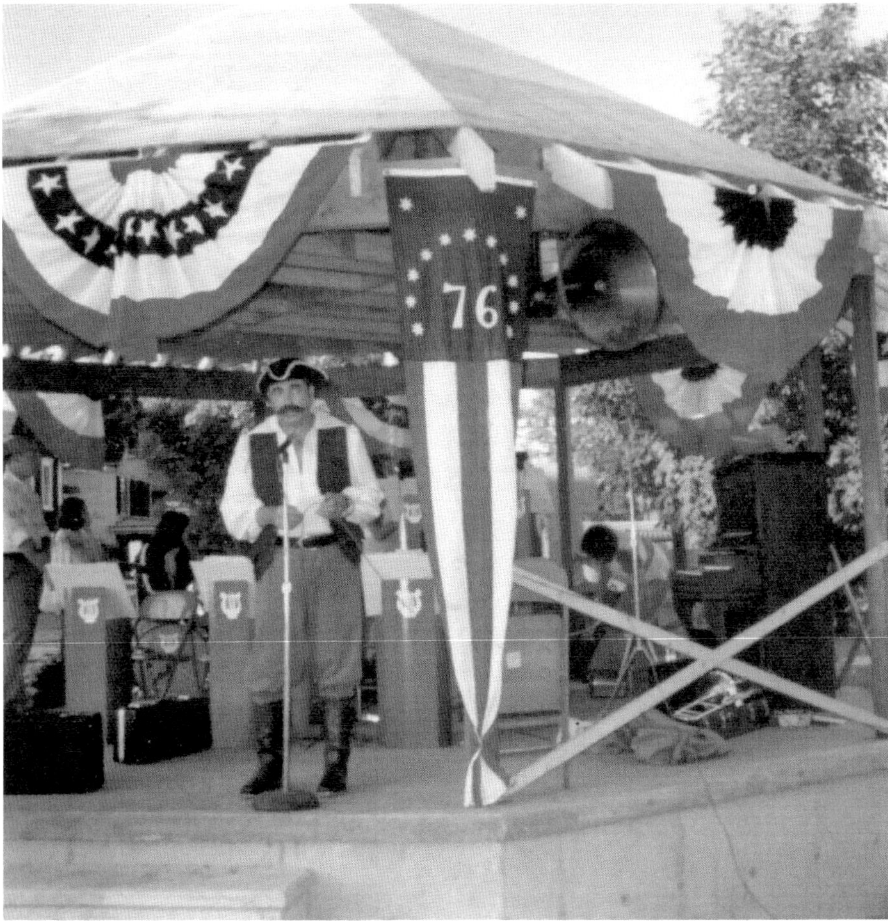

Frank Case, chair of the National Bicentennial Celebration, 1976. *Courtesy of Sally Paradis.*

many townspeople who attended danced to the music of Ted and Mark Hebert's bands. Snacks and drinks were available, and a great birthday cake was presented by Eleanor Cottrell.

The Second Annual Street Fair was held July 22–25, with increased participation over the previous year and many varied programs. It was hoped that the fair would continue in future years as a permanent carry-over from the celebration of 1976.

On July 24, one of the finest and possibly the largest parades in Raymond's history, assembled by Ted Welch and his parade committee, got underway. It took just under two hours to pass the reviewing stand.

A beautiful bicentennial quilt depicting places of historical interest in the town of Raymond was made by a group of Raymond ladies under the direction of Caroline Severance. It was presented to the Raymond Historical Society, where it remains on display today.

July 1, 1976, marked the pouring of the foundation for a permanent bandstand on the Common, and proved to be the most time-consuming project of the bicentennial year, as work was done on a voluntary basis over a period of several months. The main director (and worker) of this project was Roger Paradis, without whose aid there wouldn't have been a bandstand project. Giving time to this project were Richard Bilodeau, Gordon Cammett, Frank Case, Warren Clifford, Lawrence Cottrell, Cliff Goodwin, Norris Gove, Eugene Goddard, Paul Gustavson, William Harmon, Louis Lessard, George Treantafel and Kevin Waldron. On Saturdays and Sundays when work continued all day, lunches were served by Priscilla Perkins, Eleanor Cottrell and Peg Case. Even before the bandstand was completed, a well-attended two-hour concert was presented by the Epsom Band on September 1.

It was a very gratifying year for the committee due to the large number of people who helped and the "special spirit" generated at the time of the celebration. Projects such as this, if successful, depend not on one person, one organization or one committee, but on the dedicated work and participation of the whole community. Raymond received this participation as it joined in saying "Happy Birthday America" to our great nation in 1976.

225th Anniversary Celebration, July 1989

By Sally L. Paradis, General Committee Co-Chair

The 1988 town meeting approved the appointment of a general committee to plan an appropriate celebration in honor of Raymond's 225th anniversary. Members appointed to the general committee included Frederick (Ted) Welch and Sally Paradis, co-chairmen; Paula Devlin, secretary; and Timothy Louis, finance chairman. Other members were Kathy Campbell, Patricia Canfield, Deborah Conery, George Cottrell, Assunta Ege, Josiah Gordon, David Hoelzel, Cheryl Kenney, Chris Mataragas, Kathy Magoon, Francesca Morrissey, William Prince, Caroline Severance, Donald and Karen Tenney and Terri Welch.

During the next fifteen months, subcommittees were appointed, and the task of planning and executing a weeklong celebration was underway. With the appropriation of $15,000 at town meeting, fundraising efforts and generous contributions from business people and citizens alike, the planning turned into reality. The logo selected for the celebration "Innovation—Tradition—Growth" and the accompanying artwork inspired many of the week's activities.

The celebration opened on Saturday, July 8, with the Miss Raymond/Junior Miss Raymond Pageant. Held at the new Raymond High School cafetorium, the production ended with Rachel Britt being named Jr. Miss Raymond and Jane Paradis chosen as Miss Raymond. The 225th Anniversary Ball was held that evening in the new gymnasium with balloon trees and pastel-colored decorations carrying out the theme and adding to the festivities as nearly four hundred guests were treated to an evening of superb refreshments and dancing into the midnight hour.

Sunday, July 9, began with an ecumenical church service on the Common with Reverend Anthony Jarek-Glidden of the Raymond Methodist Church and Reverend Neil Iverson of the Raymond Congregational Church leading the worship service.

The Old Home Day program began at 1:00 p.m. with many participants dressed in costumes of earlier days. State and local dignitaries were introduced. Town clerk Gloria Carney read the minutes of Raymond's first town meeting in 1764. Following the program, the Senior Citizens Center hosted a luncheon for the program participants, and the Congregational Church hosted an ice cream social.

The Gove Middle School hosted the Raymond High School alumni reunion, one of the largest gatherings of RHS graduates. Many former faculty members were on hand, including John J. Callaghan, thirty-year teacher and principal, who served as master of ceremonies.

Other features during the week included the popular horse-pulling event, the bicycle shows (featuring members of the Cottrell family), square dancing, street dance, programs at local organizations and the opening of the town fair on Friday, July 14. Closing weekend events included pancake breakfasts hosted by the Cub Scouts at the VFW Hall, the Children's Carriage/Bicycle Parade, Ronald McDonald's appearance, Fun Olympics, a woodsmen competition, band concerts, the annual five-mile road race and the Chicken Barbeque hosted by the Raymond Methodist Church.

Topping activities for the last weekend was the spectacular 225th Anniversary Parade. Beginning at 1:00 p.m. on Old Manchester Road

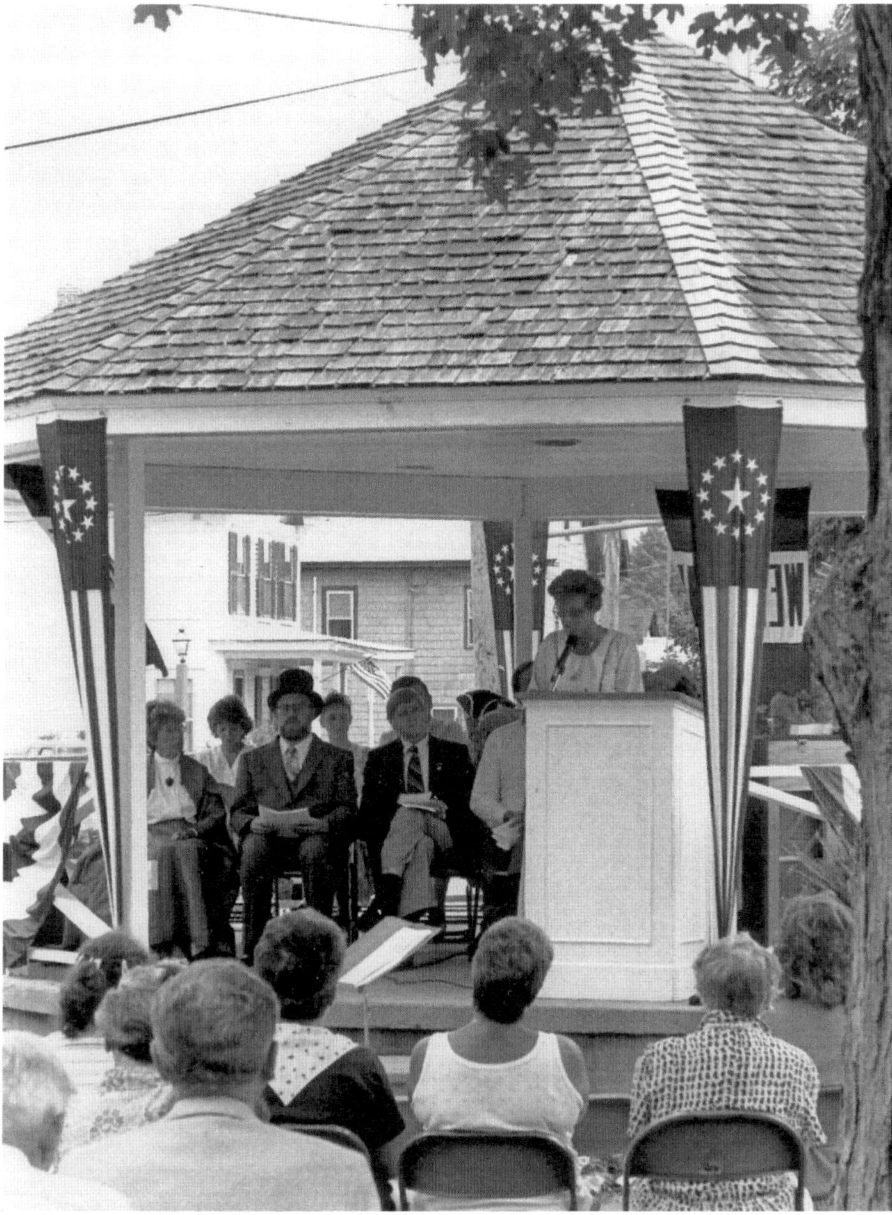

As part of the Old Home Day program, town clerk Gloria Carney read minutes of the first town meeting. *Courtesy of Sally Paradis.*

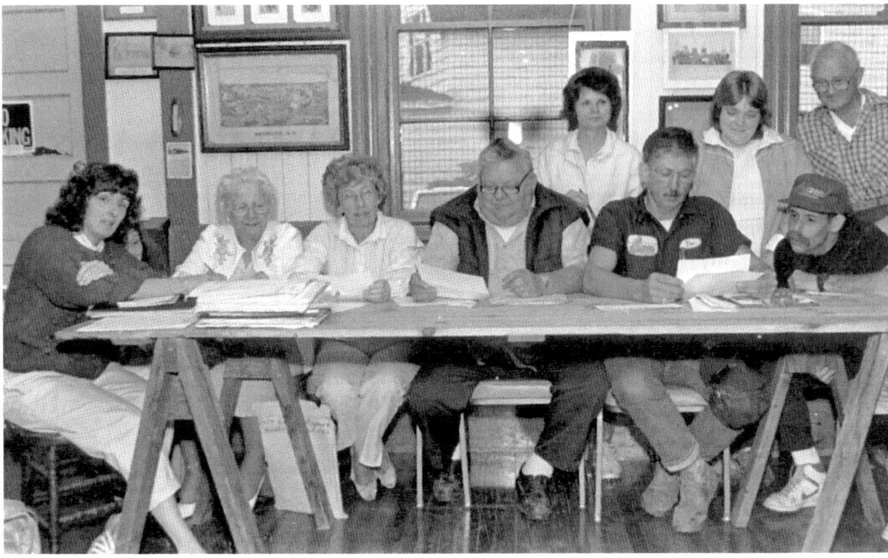

The 225th Anniversary General Committee: (front row, left to right) Paula Devlin, Caroline Severance, Sally Paradis, Ted Welch, Don Tenney and Chris Mataragas; (back row, left to right) Karen Tenney, Kathy Magoon and Bill Prince. *Courtesy of Sally Paradis.*

near Exit 4, the six-division procession of nearly one hundred units continued down Epping Street to Route 27. Led by town crier Forrest Page and followed by Grand Marshal Josiah Gordon, the two-hour parade was viewed by an estimated ten thousand people, including Governor Judd Gregg and several other dignitaries.

The 225th gala anniversary fireworks display began late Saturday evening. Silhouetted by a beautiful moon, each display was more breathtaking than the one before. Continuing for nearly an hour, the 225th anniversary fireworks were long remembered!

As a lasting memento of the occasion, the beautiful 225th anniversary quilt was displayed in the new Raymond High School. Programs and other souvenirs were made available at the Raymond Historical Society. Blessed with perfect summer weather for the entire week, a truly memorable 225th birthday for our town and its people was a success thanks to the committee's months of planning and preparing.

8

RAYMOND TOWN FAIR

BY DAVID R. HOELZEL

In 1973, the town's nonprofit organizations came together with the idea of raising funds in a collective way, rather than individually. It began with just a few organizations, including the churches, historical society and scouting troops that participated in the first July weekend event, and every year it, has gained momentum. A town fair committee was formed with at least two members from each participating nonprofit organization.

For thirty-three years, David Hoelzel (assisted by wife Kathy and family) co-chaired the annual event with Ted Welch, until Ted's passing in March 1990. In 2009, Mike Annis of the Knights of Columbus took over the reins as town fair chairman, and Steve Welch of Tucker Lodge #99 has held that post since 2012.

The requirement that participating groups not duplicate what others were featuring for games, raffles, food sales or handmade items has remained. Each organization was billed for the space it needed, as it was the desire of the committee to be self-sustaining without use of town funds. Through the efforts of Raymond Ambulance Association volunteers, little children's rides were introduced, lending a more festive feel to Raymond's "little street fair." Commercial booth spaces and larger amusements have added variety and to the fair's growth and attendance.

Recently, the town-owned lot next to the Congregational Church began being used for the amusement rides and more booths. With both sides of Church Street lined with booths and with proximity to the bandstand on the Common, this arrangement has been ideal, allowing entertainment and musical groups to perform for the enjoyment of all fairgoers.

Traditionally, the fair has kicked off with the Firemen's Parade that includes the participation of not only Raymond's fire apparatus but also that of neighboring fire departments. For several years, thanks to Ted Welch and Ray Smart, horse pulling contests were held at the old tannery site on Wight Street, where woodsmen's competitions were also held.

The children's Parade of Wheels continues to be a favorite. The sight of it leaving the school and rolling down Epping Street around the Common still puts smiles (and some tears) on the faces of onlookers! Another popular event organized by the town recreation department several years ago is the Hugh Holt road race held on Sunday that still attracts runners from throughout the New England area. For the last twenty-five years, volunteers have organized the Miss Raymond Pageant that has chosen a "Miss Raymond" to reign throughout the fair and town of Raymond activities for the following year.

The success of the fair over the years has depended largely on the electricians whose "set-up" has made it work over the years. They include Doug Hewes, Fred Richards, Dick Lahr and Sid Madore, who is still on the job! Without the help of volunteers from the participating Raymond groups and organizations and many "key friends," this unique annual town fair might not have evolved or survived for the last forty years!

9

MISS RAYMOND

BY KATHY CAMPBELL

First Miss Raymond Crowned for '64 Bicentennial

The idea of crowning a queen for the annual Winter Carnival in Raymond began in the early '40s and continued throughout the '50s. With pageants gaining more popularity state- and nationwide, the 1964 celebration featured such an event to generate interest in the town's celebration plans among the younger set. Twelve young women participated in the event headed by Queen Committee chair Shirley Dodge. The competition featured an afternoon tea held at the Pilgrim Inn with judges Robert Jolicoeur, Robert Cohen and Meg Geraghty invited from the Greater Manchester area to interview and assess each of the candidates. At the end of the afternoon, five finalists were named: Alison Welch, Judy Bouchard, Selma Reise, Inez Smith and Beverly Stetson. During the Bicentennial Ball gala the following Friday evening at Raymond High School, Selma Reise was crowned Miss Raymond.

Crowning queens didn't seem to be the fashion in Raymond again until 1983, when Cynthia Ray was chosen in an essay contest to represent the town during its annual town fair.

Miss Raymond: Twenty-five Years of Tradition

With the planning of the 225th anniversary celebration in 1989, crowning an official Miss Raymond was initiated and directed by Karen Tenney. Ten Raymond residents competed for the title of Miss Raymond and twenty-seven for Junior Miss Raymond events, which featured categories in evening and casual dress, an interview and an essay contest titled "What Raymond Means to Me." Jane Paradis was chosen to wear the first Miss Raymond crown and represented her hometown until her successor was chosen in July 1990. Rachel Britt was named Junior Miss Raymond. Both winners received scholarship funds, savings bonds, cash prizes and gift certificates from Raymond-area businesses and organizations.

Throughout the past twenty-five years, the tradition has continued with hundreds of young women in Raymond participating and being eligible to win the thousands of dollars awarded in scholarship money. Competition since the mid-'90s has included a talent category. (See the list of Miss Raymond titleholders on the next page.)

Various individuals have been pageant directors over the years, beginning with Elizabeth O'Donnell in 1991, for whom a special award is made to

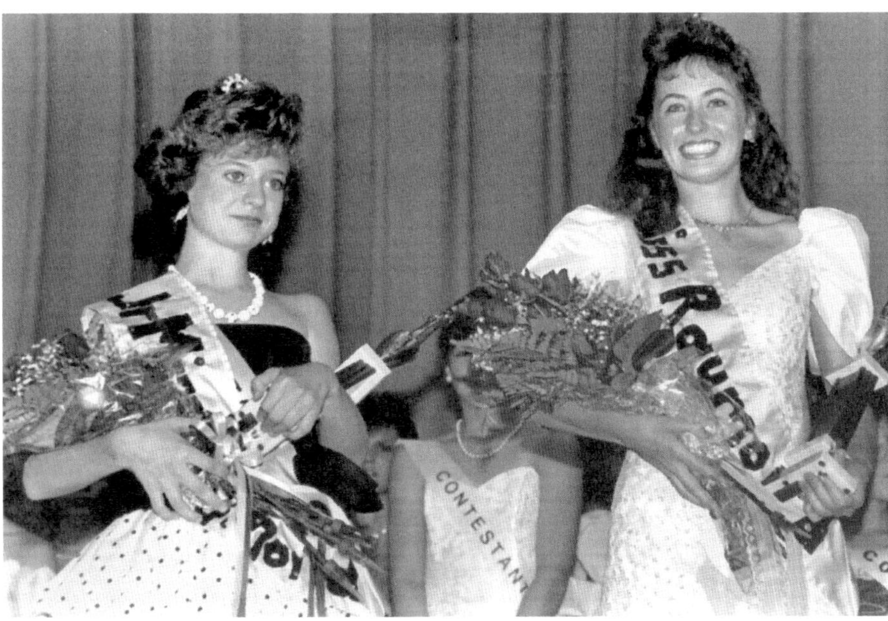

Rachel Britt, Junior Miss Raymond; Jane Paradis, Miss Raymond, 1989. *Courtesy of Sally Paradis.*

a pageant contestant each year. Directors have also included former Miss Raymond winners Sarah Jewell, Jessica Morin and Jane Paradis. Since 2007, Kathy Campbell and Lauren Campbell (first runner-up in 2006) have served as director and co-director, reinstituting the Junior Miss Raymond competition in 2006.

Taylor Brewitt, Miss Raymond 2013, and Grace Woolson, Junior Miss Raymond 2013, will relinquish their crowns to their successors in July 2014. The new winners will reign over the town's 250th celebration in September 2014.

The Miss Raymond Program has been a steppingstone for several Miss Raymond titleholders and finalists to advance to the Miss New Hampshire/ Miss America Scholarship Program. Some of these women are Lindsey Graham, Miss New Hampshire 2009; Jessica Morin, Miss New Hampshire first runner-up 2003, finalist 2004; Jane Paradis, Miss New Hampshire third runner-up 1993 and 1994; Deborah O'Donnell, Miss New Hampshire finalist 1994; Lauren Campbell, Miss New Hampshire top-ten finalist 2013.

1989: Jane Paradis
1990: Deborah O'Donnell
1991: Kelly Hurd
1992: Tanya Coll
1993: Tara Greenaway
1994: Sarah Jewell
1995: Jessica Morin
1996: Abbi Rollins
1997: Lisa Duda
1998: Jillian Burton
1999: Andrea Lee Strassner
2000: *No pageant held*
2001: Julianne Morin
2002: Candice Ducharme
2003: Lindsey Graham
2004: Stephanie Morin
2005: Heather Weghorst
2006: Lauren Campiglio
2007: Nikki Hammond
2008: Michaela Lowman
2009: Kaitlyn Edwards
2010: Valerie Dancewicz
2011: Sabrina Vail
2012: Madison Douzanis
2013: Taylor Brewitt

10

WORLD WAR II, KOREAN CONFLICT AND VIETNAM ERA MEMORIALS

BY SALLY PARADIS

On November 11, 1983, the following people met to discuss appropriate memorials to veterans of World War II, the Korean Conflict and the Vietnam Era: Frederick "Ted" Welch, commander of American Legion Post #90; Timothy Quinn, commander of VFW Maple-Wheadon Post #4479; Sally Paradis, board of selectmen representative; and John "Jack" Barnes, community member.

At this meeting, the criteria for including names on the memorial were discussed, and the following was agreed on: The veteran was to have resided in Raymond at the time of entrance to active duty, have been separated under honorable conditions and have served during the war periods established in state statutes as follows: World War II from December 7, 1941, to December 31, 1946; Korean Conflict from June 25, 1950, to January 31, 1955; Vietnam Era from December 22, 1961, to May 7, 1975.

Discussion was held as to the type of memorial and where in the town Common it could be accommodated. Working with McGann Bronze Company of Cambridge, Massachusetts, the group decided on the idea of mounting bronze plaques around the base of the bandstand (dedicated in 1976 to all veterans). The plaques were to be placed on the three façades nearest the flagpole, one for each war containing the combatants' names in lettering a quarter of an inch high and stars to designate those "killed in action."

An announcement of the project was made at an American Legion program on December 7, 1983. Fundraising began in February 1984 with letters sent to businesses, local organizations and residents. Target date for installation was Memorial Day 1984. The cost of the plaques, raised entirely by citizens, businesses, service organizations, veterans, families and friends, was $6,124. Installation of the plaques was completed by community volunteers.

The task of collecting names for the plaque was underway. The "Roll of Honor" kept on display in the post office during World War II contained nearly all of the 146 names needed. (Note: This number represented over 10 percent of Raymond's population of just over 1,300 residents in the mid-'40s.)

Researching the Korean Conflict and Vietnam veterans required the most extensive time, as no local listings were available. The Office of Adjutant General and the National Archives and Records Service in Washington, D.C., provided valuable assistance, as did citizens Nelson Sherman, Chris (Kip) Mataragas and Kent Clock, who assisted the committee for the Vietnam memorial. Lists of veterans' names were submitted to local newspapers over a period of several months, appealing to residents for verification or further information. Over the last decade, additional veterans names, based on the criteria established, have been added to the plaques.

World War II
December 7, 1941–December 31, 1946

Andrews, George H.
Armstrong, Charles N.
Barnes, Harry H.
Blanchard, Marjorie E.
Bothwick, Harold N.
Bothwick, Walter J.
Brown, Cedric, C.
Brown, George L.
Brown, Herbert W. *
Brown, Roger
Brusso, Charles H.
Cammett, Gordon A.
Cammett, Robert P.
Carver, A. Reed
Carver, Donald A.
Chamberlain, John W.*
Chapman, Nigal D., Jr.
Chase, Calvin F.
Clark, Stanley
Clark, Wilton B.
Clement, James C.
Clock, Herman A.
Clock, Hovey, B.
Crete, Cecil M.
Dearborn Arthur D
Dearborn, Fred B., Jr.

Dickinson, Robert B.
Downing, Frank V.
Downing, Kenneth L.
Dudley, John W., Jr.
Dudley, Warren J.
Durkee, Donald F.
Eccleston, Kenneth L.*
Edwards, George H.
Edwards, Glenn A.
Edwards, Paul F.
Edwards, Pauline I.
Edwards, Winston M.
Ege, Russell A.
Florence, Frank A.
Fogg, Donald
Fogg, Frank L.
Fowler, Charles H.
French, Willis C.
Gagne, Henry J.
Gagne, Oscar J.
Gill, Sumner,
Grace, Joseph R.
Gratton, Raymond J.
Griffin, Erwin C.
Griffin, Louis E., Jr.
Guyette, Frank E.
Harmon, George E.
Harmon, William W.
Hanson, Hardy L.
Harrington, Russell W.
Hayes, Kenneth H.
Hilchey, John D.
Holt, Hughin D.
Howard, Roland W.
Hupe, Albert F.
Hurd, Palmer T.
Hurd, William B., Jr.
Ingalls, Austin H.
Ireland, John D.
Knowlton, Harry L., Jr.
Lacouture, Florence B.
Lafrenier, Albert E.
LeBlanc, Ralph S.
Leighton, George C.
Levesque, Romeo E.
Lyman, Walter E., Jr.
Mafera, Frank J., Jr.
Mafera, Richard G.
Mataragas, Chris*
Mataragas, James R.
Mataragas, William
Maynard, Harry E.
McHarg, Lawrence H.
McHarg, Richard M.
Monroe, Donald W.
Moody, James
Moulton, Edward W.
Nee, John W.
Orfield, Gerhard W.
Orfield, Karl V.
Orfield, Richard A.
Ostrander, Frank O.
Page, Forrest H.
Page, Harriet G.
Paquette, Carlton I.
Paquette, Louis A.
Paquette, Richard I.
Parker, David D.
Peaslee, William E.
Pitman, Everett C.
Plante, Frederick J.
Price, David G.
Prince, William T.
Quimby, Charles C.
Quintal, Adelard L.
Quintal, Emile R.
Quintal, Rodolph, Jr.
Raymond, Floyd W.
Reed, Ivan C., Jr.
Rioux, Albert
Rioux, Robert L.
Robbins, Clarence G.

Robinson, Burgess J.
Robinson, Ernest M.
Rock, Frank W.
Rollins, Calvin C.
Rollins, Russell I.
Rollins, William L.
Shepard, Samuel M.
Simano, Harry P.
Sinclair, Harry G.
Smart, Edgar E.
Smart, Ralph C.
Smart, Raymond M.
Smith, Charles F.
Smith, Paul G.
Smith, Richard C.
Sprague, Albert A.
Sprague, George R.
Stanyon, Frank S.
Sweeney, Harold I.
Taylor, Joseph E.
Taylor, Leonidas E.
Taylor, Richard A.
Thompson, Edward A.
Tilton, John E., Jr.
Tilton, Ralph H.
Traver, Gordon A.
Traver, Paul C.
Traver, Selma I.
Underhill, Dexter
Vezina, Pauline E.
Wallace, Bernard A.
Wallace, Francis O.
Wallace, Herman E.
Wallace, Roland O.
Watt, Leonard A.
Welch, Bernard J.
Welch, Loren N.
Wheadon, Elmer D.*
Willey, Kenneth O.

*Killed in Action

Korean Conflict June 25, 1950–January 31, 1955

Baker, David C.
Barnes, Clayton D.
Barnes, Eugene A.
Beachey, Paul F.
Bernier, Gary P.
Broman, Howard C.
Brouillard, Joseph G.
Brown, Howard
Brown, Paul E.
Cate, Carl W., Jr.
Cate, Myron W.
Chapman, Nigal D., Jr.
Chase, Calvin F.
Cooley, Daniel H.
Cooley, John S.
Dahlstrom, Carl H.
Dodge, Sumner W., Jr.
Desilets, Norman C.
Dickenson, David W.
Donovan, Sheila J.
Downing, Stuart C.
Drew, Floyd I.
Dudley, Rogers E.
Dudley, Warren J.
Eaton, Franklin D.
Eaton, Grover R.
Eaton, Peter P.
Edwards, Glenn A.
Edwards, Pauline I.
Ferry, Guy M., Jr.

Fogg, Frank L.
Gagne, Romeo H.
Glidden, Dwight A.
Gordon, Andrew J., Jr.
Gordon, Richard
Greenwood, Francis D.
Greenwood, J. Henry
Greenwood, Wilfred J.
Guyette, Frank E.
Guyette, Richard E.
Guyette, Willis T., Jr.
Hartford, Frederick F., Jr.
Higgins, Douglas R.
Houle, James F.
Houle, Richard E.
Kendall, Wayne F.
Leonard, Walter J.
Lord, Charles A.
MacLaren, Robert W.
Maynard, Richard E.
Maynard, Russell W.
McHarg, Richard M.
Mullin, William F.
Newell, Albert H., Jr.
Newell, Eli N.
Nielsen, Ronald H.
Philbrick, Douglas J.
Philbrick, Keith H.
Proulx, J. Arthur
Quintal, Ernest A.
Quintal, Maurice L.
Quintal, Paul D.
Raymond, Floyd W.
Raymond, Robert R.
Reagan, Edward
Reed, Carl A.
Reed, Orrin C.
Richard, Robert L.
Robinson, Burgess A.
Robinson, Thomas J.
Rollins, A. Warren
Rollins, Robert R.
Ryan, Joseph I., Jr.
Shepard, Stanley R.
Slaughter, Paul D.
Smith, Donald H.
Taylor, Joseph E.
Taylor, Paul M.
Titus, Wendell F.
Tilton, John E., Jr.
Traver, Paul C.
Waterhouse, John F.
Welch, Frederick S.
Willoughby, Donald R.
Willoughby, Norman B.

VIETNAM ERA
December 1961–May 7, 1975

Armstrong, Gilbert C.
Arnold, Rex W.
Arnold, Ronn J.
Aston, Bruce A.
Bishop, Melvin H.
Bohle, John H.
Bouchard, Jerry A.
Boulton, James B.
Boyd, Robert D.
Broman, John H.
Brown, Charles A.
Brown, Dana L.

Brown, George C.
Brown, Reginald H.
Brown, Ronald F.
Brown, Thomas G.
Brusso, Timothy K.
Bryant, Pary P.
Cate, John C.
Chapman, Nigal D., Jr.
Clark, Harold B.
Clark, Stanley E.
Clock, David P.
Clock, Kent T.
Cross, Warren C.
Cottrell, George E.
Davis, Richard F.
Davis, Robert W.
Dionne, Jimmy R.
Downing, James F.
Downing, Kenneth L., Jr.
Drew, Floyd I.
Dudley, Delmar D.
Dudley, Duane, D.
Edwards, Glenn A.
Edwards, Pauline I.
Edwards, Winston M., Jr.
Elliott, Robert T., Jr.
Erwin, David M.
Erwin, Edward H.
Feeney, Kevin F.
Fogg, Frank L.
French, Russell A.
French, Willis C., Jr.
Fugere, Michael P.
Fugere, Oliver, Jr.
Gagne, Jerry L.
Gagne, Romeo H.
Gilcash, Stanley A., Jr.
Goldsmith, Calvin N.
Gordon, Dana L.
Gordon, Richard
Greenwood, Frederick M.
Greenwood, Robert C.
Hayes, Thomas K.
Hayes, William H.
Healey, Robert O.
Healey, Ronald A.
Henderson, Joseph E.
Hodgkins, Mark A.
Johnson, Howard
Keddy, James W., Jr.
Keddy, Michael L.
King, David J.
Launier, Arthur G.
Launier, Leo V.
Launier, Raymond
Launier, Robert H.
Levasseur, Philip G.
Levesque, Ronald C.
Longazel, John W.
Ludden, Joel E.
Malette, Arthur R.
Margaritis, Sotorios M.*
Maynard, John
Maynard, Russell W.
McGall, Thomas W.
McGovern, William F., Jr.
McKinnon, Michael K.
Moland, Richard H.
Monroe, David
Mulligan, Hugh D.
Newell, Albert H., Jr.
Newell, Eli A.
Newell, Mervin E.
Newell, Royal L.
Noel, Ernest H., III
Noel, Gary
Palmer, Walter L.
Pettengill, Michael V.

Pitkin, Albert H.
Pitkin, Kenneth F.
Plante, Lawrence J.
Prince, Warren T.
Quinn, John J.
Reagan, Edward
Reed, Ivan C., III
Reed, Michael J.
Robinson, Edward R.
Robinson, Richard A.
Robinson, Thomas J.
Rousseau, Roland L.
Ryan, Joseph I., Jr.
Ryan, Thomas P.
St. Martin, Thomas J.
Schou, John T., III
Sherman, Nelson, E.
Smart, Raymond M., Jr.
Smith, Donald C., Jr.
Spinazzola, Frank J.
Strandell, Donald J.
Tilton, John E., Jr.
Titus, Harold N., Jr.
Traver, Paul C.
Treantafel, George A.
Turner, Ronald D.
Turner, Steven J.
Waldron, Patricia C.
Wallace, Dale B.
Wallace, Donald L.
Wallace, George W., Jr.
Warthen, James W.
Warthen, Joel W.
Welch, George B.
Welch, Suzette M.
Wilbur, Everett E.
Witham, Leon R.

*Killed in Action

World War II and Korean Conflict Memorial Dedications

By Sally Paradis

The final proofs were submitted to McGann Bronze on April 4, and the plaques were delivered to Raymond the week before Memorial Day. Volunteers had labored throughout the month to prepare the façade to accept the plaques. Due to the need for extensive research and the larger number of names, dedication of the Vietnam memorial would be postponed until July 8 during town fair weekend.

Memorial Day 1984 dawned under a wet, gray sky, but the dedication went forward as planned. The World War II plaque was unveiled by Mrs. Constantina Mataragas, Raymond's only remaining Gold Star Mother from World War II, assisted by Gordon A. Cammett Sr., World

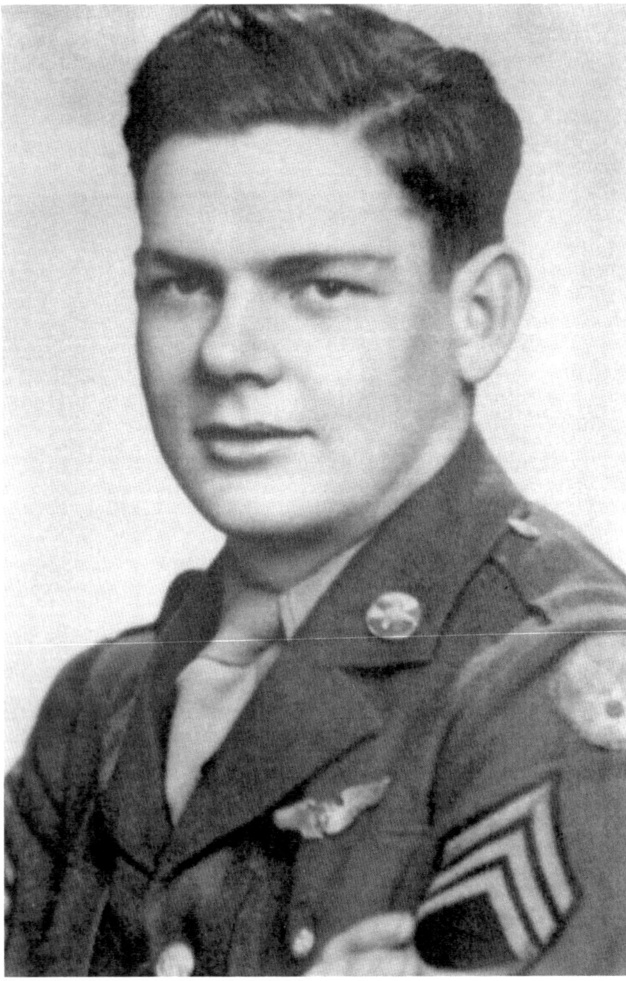

Elmer Wheadon, Raymond's first casualty of World War II. *Courtesy of Sally Paradis.*

War II veteran and former Raymond selectman. Doing the honors for the Korean Conflict plaque was Frederick "Ted" Welch, veteran of the Korean Conflict, assisted by Mrs. Etta Margaritis, Gold Star Mother of the Vietnam Era. (*Note: Mrs. Margaritis would not be available in July to unveil the plaque denoting that her son Sotorios Margaritis had been killed in action during the Vietnam Era.)*

Vietnam Memorial Dedication

By Sally Paradis

The long-awaited dedication of the Vietnam memorial was held on July 8. Despite three days of torrential rain preceding the day of the event, an all-out effort by community volunteers and town officials completed the necessary preparations. The concrete bases were constructed, concrete poured and all three plaques installed. The bandstand area was landscaped, and finishing touches added shortly before the dedication program began at 2:00 p.m. on a hot July afternoon. Governor and Mrs. John Sununu led the procession of dignitaries, including Raymond's representatives to the New Hampshire House and Senate, from the VFW post home to the Common. Greg Margaritis, brother of Sotorios Margaritis, who was killed in action, unveiled the Vietnam memorial plaque assisted by the governor.

Veterans' Memorial Bandstand Refurbished and Rededicated, June 2001–July 2002

By Paul Brown

With the passing of twenty-five years since its construction, the bandstand showed need for repair and improvement. Jack Barnes and Sally Paradis, having an interest in this structure, volunteered to work on the project in conjunction with Public Works director Dennis McCarthy.

Work areas were identified: restoring the bandstand foundation with a new coat of concrete, replacing the ceiling of the bandstand with new recessed lighting and installing an electrical panel between ceiling and roof to allow access from bandstand, improving the drainage bandstand floor by sloping the floor and installing necessary drains, installing new railings and improving the support of the structure and bringing the railing up to code using vinyl balusters to facilitate routine cleaning and maintenance.

Public opinion was solicited through an article in the *Rockingham News* showing a design similar to the bandstand in Plaistow. What few comments were received were favorable and the Historic District Commission gave its approval on June 12, 2001. Jewett Construction supplied materials for the project. Rededication of the Veterans' Memorial Bandstand and the placing of a plaque officially designating the bandstand as the Veterans' Memorial Bandstand was part of the July 4, 2002 ceremony, with senate president Arthur Klemm and state senator John "Jack" Barnes doing the honors. Roger Paradis, who constructed the original bandstand with volunteer help in 1976 and who did the restoration work in 2002, was recognized for his efforts.

Soldiers and Sailors Monument Restoration

By Paul Brown

The Soldiers and Sailors Monument, also known as the Civil War statue, was dedicated in 1910 to Raymond soldiers who fought in the Civil War, then known as the "Great Rebellion." It is a Union soldier, facing south, to discourage any would-be Confederates from attacking this tough little town.

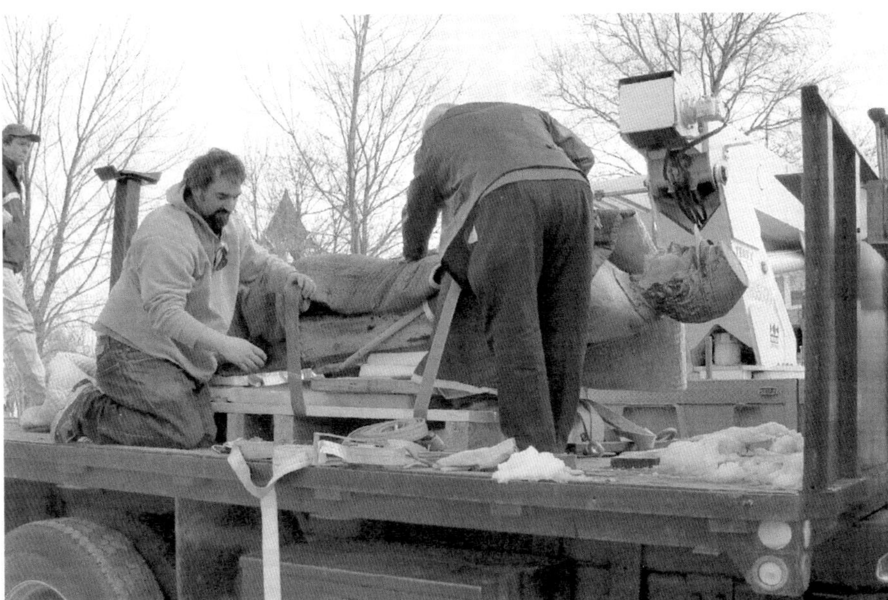

The Soldiers and Sailors Monument on its restoration journey. *Courtesy of Paul Brown.*

The monument has been a constant on the Common since then, but some misguided soul, perhaps a Confederate sympathizer, chose to shoot a hole in our warrior's bronze shoulder.

The wound festered for some thirty years, with indifferent birds building their nests in its cavity. In the late 1990s, a warrant article was proposed to appropriate the sum of $35,000 for repair and restoration of the statue. The article was defeated.

Enter Franklin Bishop, a Korean War veteran, several times selectman and state representative, along with the American Legion and Veterans of Foreign Wars, and a campaign was initiated to raise the money by private donations.

A total of $26,000 was raised, and the remaining balance came from a $10,000 grant from the New Hampshire Division of Historical Resources.

The unveiling was on Memorial Day 2005. Joshua Jonathan Schwalb, a great-great-grandson of Lieutenant John E. Cram, a Raymond hero of the Civil War, did the honors.

11

GOVERNANCE

Legislative Body

By Sally Paradis

The legislative body of the town (voters) conducted its first town meeting (including the raising and appropriating of funds) in 1764. Town meetings were to be conducted in this "traditional" manner for the next 238 years, ending in 2002. In March of that year, the town voted to adopt the provisions of the official ballot voting legislation enacted in 1995, which the school district had adopted five years earlier. Such legislation provides for a first (deliberative) session allowing for articles to be discussed, debated and amended with a second (voting) session for all articles in the warrant to be voted on at town meeting election day in March.

Board of Selectmen, Town Manager

By Sally Paradis

Governance of the town of Raymond remained in the hands of a three-member board of selectmen, in accordance with New Hampshire statutes from 1764 into the mid-1980s. With the rapid increase in population throughout the '60s and '70s, administrative handling of town affairs began to receive closer scrutiny and change was being discussed. As early as 1973, a group of citizens advanced the concept of adopting the town manager form of government. This topic was debated throughout the '70s (in 1974, 1976 and 1977). Public opinion, however, was not ready to support the measure. In 1979, the position of administrative assistant was instituted by the board of selectmen to assist it in the day-to-day coordination and delivery of services to Raymond citizens. While the position of administrative assistant improved the communication and coordination of the town's administrative services, it did not address the growing demands on the three members of the board of selectmen to act as ex-officio members of the increasing number of committees and boards being adopted at this time; i.e., the Municipal Budget Committee, Planning Board and Board of Adjustment, Conservation and Recreation. The board at that time was also actively involved in providing the leadership to resolve the town's landfill closure and other solid waste issues and for an expansion of town facilities for police, fire, dispatch and ambulance services, which, at that time, were all housed in the original fire station on Epping Street. In 1985, on a petition of 2 percent (and more) of registered voters, as required by state statute, the voters were asked to increase the board of selectmen from three to five members. The change was voted in the affirmative.

With the retirement of administrative assistant Dana Kingston in 1989, the proposal of adopting the town manager form of government was on the warrant for the 1988 town meeting. Needing more than a five-man board of selectmen could provide on a part-time basis and with more legal oversight than an administrative assistant could provide, a citizen-led petition was placed in the town meeting warrant in 1988 to "adopt the Town Manager plan as provided in Chapter 37 of the Revised Statutes Annotated" and was voted in the affirmative, leading to a change in the oversight of town employees and the delivery of town services.

Raymond's first town manager, appointed in 1989, was Martha St. Amand. Under her direction, the town was awarded a Community

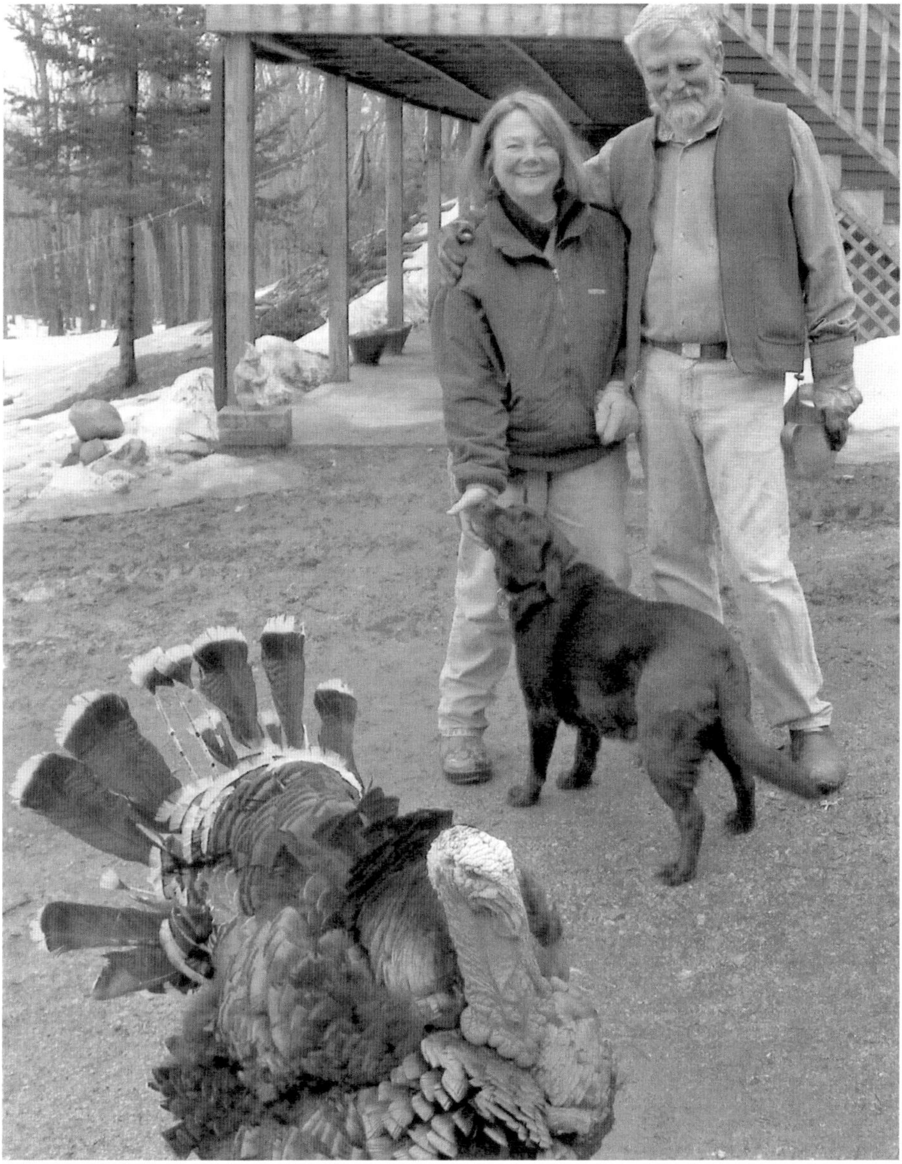

Town manager Craig Wheeler and Donna Wheeler with their dog, Lola, and turkey, Waldo.
Courtesy of Paul Brown.

Development Block Grant to improve the downtown area into the '90s, with sidewalk reconstruction in the Main and Church Street areas, new fencing for the Common and landscaping. She also acted as the town's welfare administrator.

At the same time, Raymond and surrounding communities in southeastern New Hampshire were experiencing unparalleled growth and were beginning to look more closely at the pros and cons of elected versus appointed department heads. The question of whether an elected department head answered to direction from a board of selectmen even though he or she would be elected by the voters became increasingly routine. Courts generally held that even though a department head would be directly elected by the people, supervision and direction was in the hands of the board of selectmen. Raymond's town warrant in 1979 asking for an appointed chief of police failed; however, another in 1981 was approved by the voters. The position of an appointed Road Agent was approved in 1982.

In the early '80s, state statutes were amended to allow for a three-year (rather than a one-year) term for town clerk, tax collector and town treasurer. Raymond voters approved such a measure in 1983.

In 2006, Warrant Article 46 was passed by the voters requiring the town manager to be a resident of the town. An adequate number of applicants were not deterred by the rule.

In 2012, Craig Wheeler, who had worked in Raymond previously as a planner, was selected as town manager. He moved with his wife, Donna, from Portsmouth.

Both Mr. and Mrs. Wheeler have embraced Raymond and are guiding members of the 250th committee. They have adapted to the farm life, growing their own produce, fashioning a sophisticated sap-boiling system and raising chickens. A gigantic turkey named Waldo has escaped the Thanksgiving roasting pan and enjoys guiding visitors about the yard.

Ethics Committee

By Pamela Turcotte

The Raymond Ethics Committee is made up of five elected members serving three-year terms. The Ethics Committee is not set up to be the "prosecutor of wrongdoing," nor is it to be considered the "Ethics Police."

The Ethics Committee has two main objectives: to serve as quasi-judicial mediators between the general public and public servants and to train public servants with regard to the Raymond Code of Ethics. The ethics code was established in 2003.

The Ethics Committee meets on the second Tuesday of each month at Raymond High School. If a second meeting is needed, it will meet on the fourth Tuesday at the same location. Meetings generally start at 6:30 p.m. and are televised by RCTV on Channel 22.

Some of the major accomplishments of the committee are:

- Development of user-friendly inquiry and complaint forms.
- Education of boards, volunteers and employees of the Town of Raymond
- Development of a procedure to process inquiries and complaints
- Development of a consistent procedure for pre-hearing and hearings.

The Ethics Committee can be reached by e-mail, which is set up independently from that of the Town of Raymond to ensure the minimizing of conflicts of interest. The e-mail address is raymondnhethicscommittee@yahoo.com. The committee's telephone number is 895-4735, ext. 220.

The Ethics Committee is set up to handle all public inquiries and/or complaints. By definition an inquiry is simply a question regarding a process or procedure that may possibly be at issue. A complaint is the formal "charging" of potential wrongdoing or conflict of interest. Anyone filing a complaint must have exhausted all avenues of recourse prior to lodging a complaint with the Ethics Committee.

The meeting minutes are available at the town hall as prescribed by RSA 91-A. The minutes are also available on the Town of Raymond website at www.raymond-nh.com. The committee's members are Jerry Zimmel, Cheryl Killam, Gretchen Gott, Joyce Wood and Michael O'Donnell. Alternate is Richard Flibotte.

Historic District Commission

By Ernest Creveling

The town of Raymond's Historic District Commission (HDC) was established in 1992 by a vote of the Raymond Town Meeting. The first historic district was approved by voters in the 1970s and included the Boston & Maine Railroad Depot land and buildings, owned by the Raymond Historical Society. The original members of the Raymond Historic Commission, as appointed in 1992, are Tim Louis, chairman; Richard Allen, vice-chairman; Elaine Harmon; Barbara Keefe; Caroline Severance; Assunta Ege; and Ramona Stevens

The Raymond Historical Commission's inaugural meeting was held on July 22, 1992, at which time the above officers were elected.

It is apparent from the meeting minutes of 1992 that the Historic District Commission members took their charge seriously, as they researched and invited guest speakers from neighboring towns to share with them how they promoted their districts and worked to preserve them.

During the years of 2000 and 2001, several properties were added to the Historic District Overlay Zone, known as Zone F in the Raymond Zoning Ordinance. The following land and structures compose Raymond's Historic Overlay District as it exists today.

Tax Map	Lot	Address	Common Reference
27-2	29	10 Main Street	former severance property
27-2	30	12 Main Street	former cobbler shop *(03/01)*
27-2	55	7 Main Street	Maclaren residence *(03/01)*
28-1	47	28 Main Street	former Welch Oil Co. *(03/01)*
28-3	58	1 Old Manchester Road	former doctor's office
28-3	59	Main Street and Old Manchester Road	Jewett Elderly Housing *(03/01)*
28-3	68	51 Main Street	Methodist Church *(03/01)*
28-3	79	2 Epping Street	Brewitt Funeral Home
28-3	80	4 Epping Street	town office complex
28-3	81	8 Epping Street	Sovereign Bank
28-3	82	Epping and Main Streets	town Common

28-3	86	9 Epping Street	Pilgrim Inn Apartments *(03/00)*
28-3	88	5 Church Street	Congregational Church *(03/00)*
28-3	89	Church Street	Howard buildings *(03/00)*
28-3	90	56 Main Street	Howard buildings *(03/00)*
28-3	91	58 Main Street	Howard buildings *(03/00)*
28-3	95	Main Street	former railroad depot

Source: Raymond Zoning Ordinance

The Historic District Commission is responsible for reviewing proposed changes to any property within the district. Upon the completion of a successful review, the commission votes to issue a certificate of approval for any alterations. An example of this process is reflected in the minutes of May 17, 2007, during which the commission considered after-the-fact alterations to 10 Main Street. Ultimately, because the applicant, who had already made repairs and alterations, did so after researching and attempting to match historic photos of the building, the commission was able to issue a certificate of approval.

On May 1, 2008, the Historic District Commission approved an application from the Congregational Church of Raymond for a restoration project involving new siding, painting and window, sill, trim and turret work.

On June 22, 2010, a certificate of approval was issued for the reconstruction of the ramp and platform leading to the boxcar at the B&M Railroad Depot, which is owned by the Raymond Historical Society and which is the only property on the National Register of Historic Places.

On occasions in 2010 and 2011, the HDC also considered and ultimately approved the reroofing of the Dudley-Tucker Library and renovation of the deck to the main entrance from Epping Street, respectively.

Over the past two years, the HDC has undergone a rebirth of sorts. For various reasons, the commission membership dwindled and there was confusion about whose terms were expired and how to reappoint membership. During 2013, the remaining members worked with the selectmen to rejuvenate the commission with new members, and the reenergized group has begun to research methods to improve oversight and visibility of its historic district. Current members are:

- David Hoelzel, chair
- Diane White, vice-chair
- Joyce Wood, secretary
- Sally L. Paradis
- Assunta Ege
- Diane Debruyckere
- Dean Plender, alternate
- Richard Lamarre, alternate
- James Levesque, alternate
- Wayne Quintal, alternate
- Greg Bemis, board of selectman representative
- Peter Buckingham, board of selectmen, alternate representative

Raymond Community Television (RCTV)

By Kevin Woods

In 1997, the Raymond Board of Selectmen entered into an agreement with Media One of New England to provide cable television services to its residents. Steve Keith, a resident, volunteered to help negotiate that contract. At that time, many local-origin channels that used to be run by the cable providers were being transitioned into PEG (Public, Educational and Government) Access facilities that were run by each municipality using franchise fee payments made by the cable providers. In Raymond, it was decided that a group of volunteers would run the access station, so Steve reached out to Kevin Woods and Marc Vadeboncoeur, both residents with professional television experience, to assist. Eventually, the town created a Cable TV Committee. Members, now numbering seven, are appointed by the selectmen to a three-year term.

As part of the negotiations with Media One, the town received a capital equipment grant of $50,000 and a franchise fee of 2 percent of the gross annual revenue received by Media One from subscribers. A space was located in the present town office building, and equipment was acquired from state and federal surplus offices, New Hampshire Public Television, and wherever else Marc, Steve and Kevin could get it. The town office meeting room was equipped with robotic cameras and microphones to record meetings. An agreement was entered into with the Raymond School District to take over a media storage room as a control room/office and to share an adjacent classroom as a studio. Much of the initial grant from Media One was put into the renovations and equipment for this studio. The selectmen of the time voted to allocate all cable related franchise fees to the operation of Raymond Community Television. It was agreed that no other funds from taxpayers would be used to pay for RCTV expenses.

In 1999, Media One was bought out by AT&T, and in 2003, Comcast took over the franchise agreement from AT&T. RCTV volunteers covered various board meetings and hauled equipment to the schools for the annual town deliberative sessions. Eventually, the town outgrew the town office meeting room, and town board and committee meetings were moved to the high school. RCTV relocated its master control and meeting room equipment to the studio control room/office and cabled cameras and microphones into the adjacent media center. Sometime later, the Industrial Arts room was added as a second meeting room and a console installed in an adjacent storage closet.

School events such as band and choral concerts were recorded by volunteers, as were Raymond High School graduations, Memorial Day parades and other local events. RCTV continued to grow. The cable committee remained very frugal in its use of the franchise fees, allowing it to save up for major capital purchases. Portable cameras were purchased, a second channel for public access programming was secured from Comcast and a computer editing system was installed. As the need grew, a part-time position of cable coordinator was added.

Over time, it became increasingly difficult to staff board and committee meetings with volunteers. It was decided that funds were available to pay for help with this. The committee drafted a proposal for "Government Access Media Operators" who would be paid a flat rate stipend for each meeting they covered. All funds would come from the RCTV budget. The selectmen adopted the recommendation.

In 2008, RCTV added "on-demand" streaming, which meant that people anywhere could download a meeting or school event and watch it. They did not have to live in Raymond and receive Comcast programming. In 2011, this system was improved so that viewers did not have to download the entire meeting but could watch it with a web browser at raymondtv.pegcentral.com. In 2012, the cable committee approved the purchase of equipment to allow live streaming of programming. People anywhere in the world with Internet access can now view government meetings live on the web.

A new agreement was entered into with the school district to continue to allow RCTV to occupy space in the High School. The selectmen also entered into negotiations with Comcast to renew the franchise agreement.

RCTV continues to follow its primary purpose "to permit participation and awareness of governmental and educational programming and in terms of public access to act as a resource for the expression of FREE SPEECH for those in our community." The fulfillment of that primary purpose fosters these secondary purposes:

- To be a tool for communication.
- To provide a means of entertainment and information.
- To provide a means of education of the Townspeople of Raymond.
- To foster the spirit of community.

Many volunteers have come and gone over the years, some as members of the Cable TV Committee and others devoting significant time to covering important town events.

Current Cable Committee members are Marc Vadeboncoeur (chair) Chester Goquen (vice-chair) Kathy Campbell, Kathy Masso, Debra Moore, Bruce White and Kevin Woods (cable coordinator). Past committee members and volunteers include Linda Jameson, Kathy Magoon, Ron Edgar, Mark Prescott, Jim Holmes, Bruce Flower, Joe Lucafo, Brian Campbell, Christine Eppig Creeden, Arlene French, Melissa French, Garrick Creeden, Dean Plender, Jolene Beaulieu, Russ Pomerleau, Roger Moore, Jill Vadeboncoeur, Luke Vadeboncoeur, Dana Zulager and Jonathan Wood.

Raymond Ambulance Incorporated

By Pauline Gordon

The Raymond Ambulance Fund Association was formed in March 1959 from an idea by Robert Eccleston, a local storekeeper. Ernest Cote was elected chairman of a committee to raise money to purchase a used ambulance to serve Raymond and surrounding towns. In less than a month, they collected over $2,700, purchased an ambulance and presented it to the town. In 1959,

Raymond Ambulance was formed as a private nonprofit organization with twenty-three members serving Raymond and surrounding towns.

As an all-volunteer organization, there was no billing, as it was supported by donations from individuals, towns, clubs and organizations and patients and families served.

The first ambulance purchased was a 1952 Cadillac, and it made 114 trips the first year. By 1983, Raymond Ambulance was recording over 500 trips a year and covered the towns of Raymond, Candia, Fremont, Nottingham and Deerfield.

In 1974, when the Raymond Dispatch Center was formed, the basic means of communication with ambulance personnel was via telephone and with the ambulance by radio. Members now communicate with portable radios and pagers.

In 1996, the organization now known as Raymond Ambulance Incorporated responded to 988 calls and had a membership of twenty-seven fully certified EMTs (emergency medical technicians) and first responders.

Raymond Ambulance offers classes and training for first responders, CPR and First Aid, the Vial of Life Program, Fatal Reality demonstration and the Raymond Ambulance Living Memorial Scholarship, awarded to a Raymond High School graduate continuing his or her education.

Raymond Ambulance still operates as a private, nonprofit corporation, and this year, it celebrates fifty-five years of service meeting the emergency medical needs of the community. With twenty-five members and four ambulances, it responded to 1,572 calls last year. It is staffed by volunteers and paid individuals twenty-four hours a day, seven days a week.

Raymond Fire Department

By Kevin Pratt, chief, and Crystal Pratt Bushey

Over the years, histories of the Raymond Fire Department have been authored by department members, including a compilation of department minutes by Captain David Baker and a manuscript titled "Out of the Ashes" printed in the department's 100th anniversary publication by Stephen Goldthwaite and Dale Jellison.

The 1976 history of the department concluded with the appointment of the first full-time chief, Burgess Chase, in 1973. Chief Chase served his last day in that post on July 31, 1977, recalling that one of the three largest fires during his time on the department was that of the Regis Tanning Company on Wight Street that occurred on July 16, 1972. Fire departments from ten communities fought the huge blaze, which engulfed the entire 550-foot building within thirty-five minutes. At the time, the tannery was the second-largest employer in Raymond. (Though it meant that the fifty employees were forced to seek employment elsewhere, the fire also brought an end to the business of tanning hides in the town of Raymond.)

Leslie Gatcomb succeeded Chief Chase, and thirty months later, Gordon Gould was appointed to the post. The '80s could be defined as the decade that the new Route 101 four-lane highway from Manchester to the seacoast was completed, and with it, the population of Raymond spiraled. With more homes and businesses being built, Paul Hammond was appointed assistant chief in 1986 to do home inspections and oversee the maintenance of the department's equipment, a post he still holds today. Assistant Chief Hammond is the town's longest-serving full-time firefighter as of this time.

The department moved forward with a system of house numbering years before it was to be required by higher authorities, a system that continues to be extremely helpful to all safety services. By the late '80s, space in the original Epping Street fire station was no longer adequate to accommodate personnel and equipment needed for fire, police, dispatch and ambulance services. A Safety Complex Committee was formed to study possible alternatives.

Chief Gould retired in 1987 and was succeeded by Kevin Pratt, who came from a long list of firefighters in his family, including his father, grandfather and brother, and whose daughter and son in-law have carried on the family tradition in recent years. In 1990, the department lost a third-generation fireman with the untimely death of Ted Welch, who had held every post in the department except that of chief.

At the March 1990 town meeting, voters approved a $790,000 bond issue to construct a new safety complex at the corner of Scribner and Old Manchester Roads just off Exit 4 of the new Route 101. The ground floor was to be occupied by fire, emergency management and ambulance services with access on Old Manchester Road, while police and dispatch with their own parking area and entrance to the building would be off Scribner Road. With twelve bay doors, the fire department would have one of the largest stations in the area. All safety services moved to the new location in

December 1990. The flagpole from the old fire station erected by firefighters in memory of thirty-two-year Deputy Chief Raymond Smith on May 30, 1973, was moved to the new fire station.

In July 1994, the Torrent Hose Company celebrated one hundred years of service to "fair Raymond" with a firemen's ball befitting those of earlier days held at the new station. For the occasion, a souvenir program of the department's history over the years was published.

Fire visited the center of town again on March 25, 1998, when it struck the old fruit store. When firefighters arrived at the scene, smoke was pushing out every pipe; people were still exiting the building. Though the structure was not saved, luckily the fire was contained to the one building, avoiding the disastrous fire that occurred in Raymond's downtown area in 1892.

With many firemen employed away from Raymond, the availability of volunteer firemen during the daytime hours began to diminish, and two full-time fire fighters were added to the department in 1996.

The cause of fires is often a product of Mother Nature, with seven of the fourteen structure fires in 2005 ignited by lightning strikes.

The department's Fire Explorers has held a Career Development Program for men and women ages fourteen to twenty-one who are interested in the emergency field of fire fighting and prevention. Many have gone on to become fire fighters in towns and cities throughout the state; some are now fire chiefs.

By the late '90s, the town had eighteen three-story buildings with roofs beyond reach of ground ladders. At the time Walmart was built, it was the largest flat-roof building in the state of New Hampshire with a surface of 1.2 million square feet in area. The town purchased a one-hundred-foot tower, with a generous donation from Walmart, which was put into service on May 30, 2003.

In 2000, the town passed an ordinance requiring sprinkler systems in multifamily buildings (over two units). Most businesses, apartments and all three schools are now fully sprinkled. To date, four fires have been extinguished by sprinklers, with three businesses and four lives possibly saved.

The department continues a tradition of building its own fire trucks and equipment that have served well over the years, augmenting that which the town has purchased to keep up with the latest trends in firefighting. Presently, the department houses the following equipment: three engines, a tanker, the rescue truck, the one-hundred-foot tower and three forestry vehicles. This equipment helps keep the ISO fire insurance rate low. Included are two vehicles equipped with Hurst Rescue tools, which allow two vehicle rescues

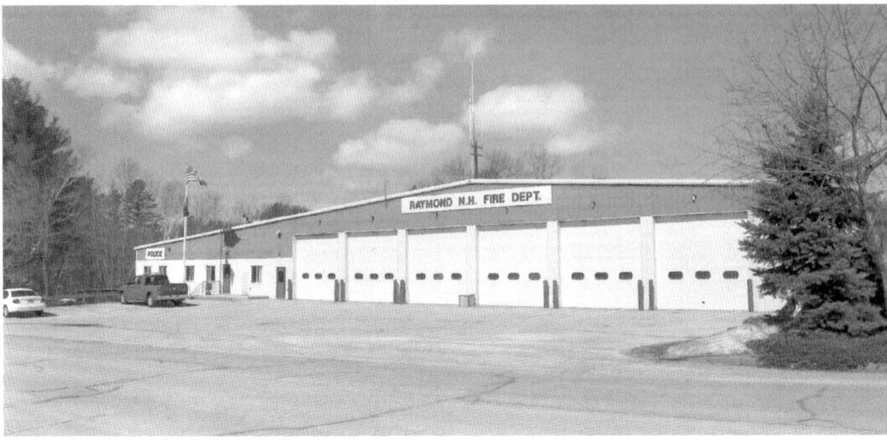

Raymond's Safety Complex *Courtesy of Paul Brown.*

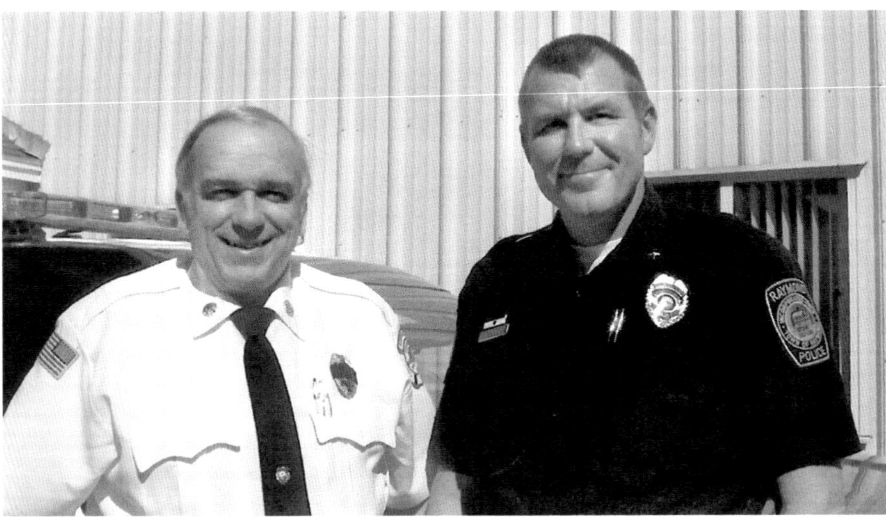

Two chiefs: Kevin Pratt, Raymond Fire Department; David Salois, Raymond Police Department. *Courtesy Paul Brown.*

at the same time. Hundreds of people have been delivered to the hospitals within the "golden hour," resulting in hundreds of lives saved since Raymond firefighters, along with Chief Chase, first saw these tools demonstrated at the Rockingham County complex during the '70s and monies were raised by the Raymond Fire Fighters Association to purchase them.

The old 1930 Maxim fire engine remains a treasure for the town and was retired in 1974 because of age, but not before pumping for three days at the tannery fire in 1972—one of its last fires. It is brought out each year to lead the Fire Fighters Parade at the town fair carrying the newly crowned Miss Raymond.

The department lost its third chaplain, Neal White, in 2013 after a long and courageous battle with cancer. Reverend White was preceded by Chaplain Chandler Newton, who held the post for several years, and by Reverend Richard Moore, the department's first.

Out of the ashes of 1892, a well-trained and well-equipped company of professionals has served the town. From those who have already needed its protection and those who hope they never will, all commend the dedication of Raymond firefighters for their service to our "fair Raymond."

Raymond Police Department

By Pauline Gordon, with Chief David Salois

Prior to 1974, the Raymond Police Department operated with a part-time chief and two part-time officers covering the town weekdays and twenty-four hours on the weekends. The department communications, using two-way radios, were handled from the chief's residence. Emergency calls for service were received through "red phones" at different locations around town. With the election of J. Henry Greenwood as the first full-time police chief, replacing Chief John Harney in 1974, a big step took place with the establishment of a twenty-four-hour dispatch center to handle the emergency communications for Raymond Police, Fire and Ambulance Departments.

The first dispatcher (part time) was Burgess "Punky" Robinson, who, with a radio background, organized the first dispatch center. Radio base stations were set up in the police room in the back of the old fire station, allowing local communications with the responding units and the ability to relay motor vehicle information from New Hampshire State Police headquarters in Concord to Raymond police officers on the road. Daily logs were handwritten and a typewriter used for department reports. Portable radios and plectron units were the mode of communication between the base and emergency personnel.

The town was growing, and by 1975, the department had expanded to four full-time officers. Chief Greenwood resigned in 1976, and Mark Long was elected police chief. In 1977, department personnel built an office in the back of the fire station to accommodate the dispatch equipment and personnel in a secure location. The dispatch center expanded operations to include the Raymond highway department as well as Fremont, Candia, Deerfield and Nottingham fire and rescue departments.

Deputy Chief Robert Elliott was the last elected chief in 1980; Richard Dolan became the first appointed police chief in 1982.

On December 20, 1990, the Police Department moved to its present location at the corner of Scribner and Old Manchester Roads with the building of the new Safety Complex facility.

In 1995, the computer systems were upgraded with the addition of the New Hampshire State Police Online Communication Systems, giving Raymond police instant access to obtain driver's license, vehicle registration and motor vehicle records from every state, as well as FBI criminal records.

With the retirement of Chief Dolan in 1994, James Murphy was appointed chief, followed by Stephen Agrafiotis in 1997 and the present chief, David Salois, in 1999.

In 1996, the department assigned its first school resource officer, Jonathan Kelly, to cover all Raymond schools during the school year.

In 2000, renovations were made to the dispatch console area to accommodate a second dispatch position, upgrading the telephone system to digital and the recording system to a digital data logger and improving the alarm-monitoring program and security cameras system.

In 2004, the department began using mobile data terminals in its cruisers, connected to the station through the Verizon Wireless network, enabling officers to run motor vehicle and license checks and complete reports from inside the cruisers.

In 2005, a complete renovation occurred in the dispatch center, modernizing all radios and associated infrastructure and replacing the consoles with "pods" that enable the dispatchers to have all the equipment combined into three computer screens in front of them. Radio systems were updated, bringing a host of new features, including panic buttons on all the cruiser/portable radios.

In 2007, the department purchased a "Code Red" program that allows the recording of an emergency message, keeping residents informed via their residential and cellular phones, as well as e-mail.

In 2013, the police department obtained a new narrow-band frequency for the fire department, replacing the seacoast fire radios and updating the system to take advantage of the two transmittal sites.

The Raymond Police Department has steadily grown from a part-time chief and a couple of part-time officers in 1974 to the present department of eighteen full-time officers, three part-time officers, a police prosecutor, an animal control officer, two civilian employees, six full-time dispatchers and two part-time dispatchers. The Dispatch Center provides communications for Raymond Police, Fire, Ambulance and Public Works Departments, along with the Fremont Fire and Rescue departments.

In 2014, a life sentence was handed down by Judge N. William Delker for a man who had committed a number of vicious sexual assaults against a family member. This is the first time a defendant was sentenced to life behind bars for a crime investigated by the Raymond Police Department.

Raymond Recreation Department

By Michelle Gordon Weaver

The Raymond Recreation Commission was officially established at the 1976 town meeting to provide year-round recreation activities, but this certainly was not the town's first steps in providing such entertainment. Actually, the Summer Playground that exists today began in the summer of 1954. About seventy-five children attended the weekly morning program, which was supported with donations by local merchants, bake sales and tag days.

The newly established Recreation Commission took over the operations of the summer program in 1976 and hired its first full-time, year-round recreation director, Rick Bates, in June 1977. Rick had a handful of part-time and seasonal staff over the next decade. He hired the first permanent part-time secretary in 1988. The part-time program assistant became a full-time assistant director in 1997, giving recreation three year-round employees that we still have today. In 2000, Rick Bates moved on to become the town manager. Michelle (Gordon) Weaver was hired as the second director in 2001.

With strong community support, the Recreation Department has blossomed into a well-rounded program for adults as well as for children. In those early days, the support of local volunteers proved crucial for the success of the program, and this still holds true today, as many people volunteer in programs run by the Recreation Department or other service-oriented organizations.

It has been one of the goals of the Recreation Department to encourage this type of cooperative community spirit by providing whatever support is necessary to help volunteers do their jobs and then filling in the spaces with our own programs. We have so many great organizations in town: Raymond Youth Athletic Association, Raymond Soccer Club, Town Fair Committee, Raymond Arts Associates, Raymond Youth Basketball, Fourth of July Parade Committee, Riverside Park Committee, Ray-Fre Senior Center, Raymond Coalition for Youth, Raymond Historical Society, NorRock Football and Cheering and Scouting for both boys and girls—all with great volunteers.

Raymond Recreation now offers and supports over two hundred programs, trips and events each year. We are also responsible for the town newsletter *On the Common*, the Annual Town Report and updating part of the bulletin board on our local cable channel. Our amazing Summer Playground is still going strong with almost three hundred participants each summer. The program has grown into two sites with a great variety of field trips, special events and daily activities.

Raymond Water Department

By Denise O'Grady

The history of the Raymond Water Works Company, Inc., from 1893 to 1976, chronicled in the *Pictorial History of Raymond, N.H.*, addressed the rapid growth during the '60s that resulted in the purchase of sixty-seven acres of land and a well from the Manchester Sand, Gravel and Cement Company, located along the B&M Railroad off Old Manchester Road, at a cost of $52,000, with repayment to be borne by the water users. (As a matter of interest, the material excavated from this area was transported by rail to Boston for the building of the Prudential Center.) This acquisition provided an excellent gravel-packed well with the capability of serving the water users for many years to come. With continued growth into the '70s, however, new demands for water were soon to be felt.

With the construction of the new Lamprey River Elementary School in 1976, a new twelve-inch main was laid along Old Manchester Road connecting the school and improving the distribution of water to Main Street.

During the mid-'80s, the proximity of neighboring homes to the town landfill off Prescott Road became a serious concern. With the closing of the landfill, a Community Development Block Grant extended town water to these homes in the Route 107 and Prescott Road area. Town water was extended to outlying areas, including Otter Road and Essex Drive, as new residential and commercial development continued.

The Raymond Water Department, since being formed in 1892, was under the direction of three elected water commissioners. An article in the 1986 warrant asked voters to place management of the Water Department under the direction of the board of selectmen, leaving the commissioners in an advisory capacity only; the article was discussed and defeated at town meeting that year. Beginning in 1989, when the town meeting adopted the town manager form of government, the Raymond Water Department fell under the direction of the town manager. In 1993, the water division received a plaque for the Orchard Street standpipe being one hundred years old, a monument to the action of the New Hampshire legislature authorizing the town to construct a water system after the disastrous fire in 1892. In 1999, the Route 156 tower was repainted with "Town of Raymond" added to the exterior.

Throughout the next decade, improvements were made to the water system. A water treatment plant was constructed by T-Buck Construction of Auburn Maine in 2003. It was designed to remove radon, iron and manganese from the source water and to add chlorine to the finished water at a cost of $1.5 million dollars, to be paid by water division revenue. Such treatment resolved the system's "brown" water problem due to a high concentration of these elements. Another 1,500 linear feet of eight- and six-inch main was constructed on Clover Court. In 2005, a 600,000-gallon concrete water tower was constructed on Long Hill Road to provide the town with additional fire flow capacity.

The water division felt the impact of floods in 2007 with the availability of department staff diminished and focused instead on maintenance issues. The 114-year-old Orchard Street tower received interior cleaning. A major water line break was addressed with the potential to drain the entire system. With rapid and effective action of the staff, the three towers were shut down, the system isolated, the leak located and service restored—however, not before nearly one million gallons of water flowed out of the system from a leak in a ten-inch line located on private property.

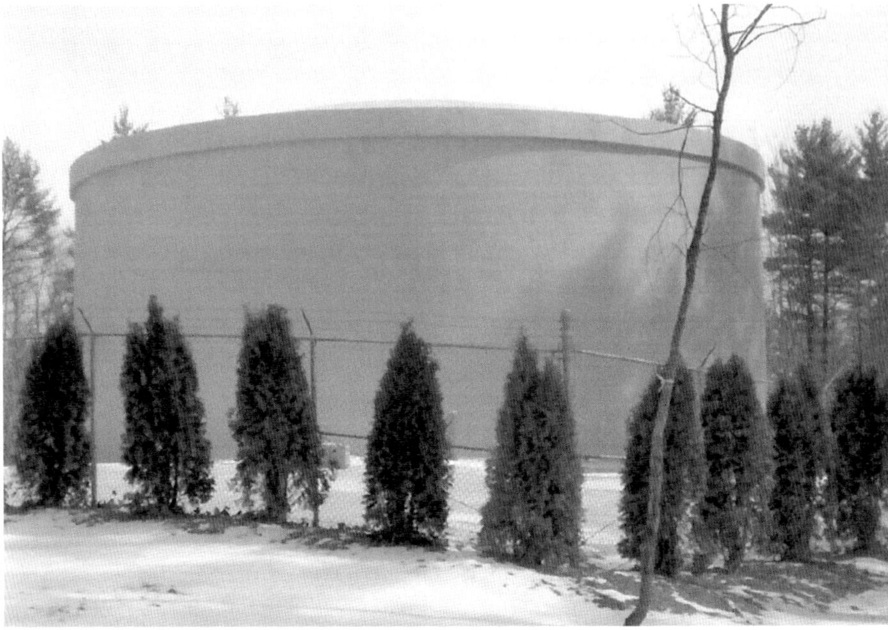

Carroll H. Huddleston Reservoir on Long Hill. *Courtesy of Raymond Water Department.*

Work on leak detection within the system continued. In the latter part of the first decade of the 2000s, the division began the process of securing a new water source on the west side of town, with test wells being installed within the Thibeault Corporation gravel pit adjacent to Route 27, with yield of the underlying aquifer being very significant. Over the last few years, the exploration for new well sites has continued throughout the town, including the Flint Hill area.

In 2013, a new water main was constructed along Route 102 to the Blueberry Hill Road site of the former Mottolo Super Fund area. Twenty-five home wells were deemed to have been contaminated. The U.S. Environmental Protection Agency and State of New Hampshire Department of Environmental Services funded the construction of the water line to service these properties with town water.

History of the Carroll H. Huddleston Memorial Reservoir

By Paul Brown

In 2003, the board of selectmen voted to purchase land on Long Hill for an additional water tower. The land was purchased from the Reverend David Cross of Mill Valley, California. Reverend Cross was a stepdescendant of the Tucker family, who had owned the property for over one hundred years. Reverend Cross kept ownership as a way of maintaining a connection with his New Hampshire roots. He preferred not to sell the property, but the town's legal counsel implied that a taking by eminent domain would be considered. Thus, the owner obliged, and the tower was built.

The town agreed to Reverend Cross's request that the tower be named after his uncle, Carroll Hyde Huddleston, an heir to the Tucker properties. Huddleston had been an engineer who had designed reservoirs in Central America and in New York State. His demise occurred while attempting a circumnavigation in a sailing vessel, chronicled in a book by Richard Maury entitled *The Saga of Cimba*.

The Meetinghouse and the Demon Rum

By Paul Brown

In the early twenty-first century, many of us get a little peeved at the slow wheels of government. We point at Democrats and Republicans and wonder why they can't agree on anything.

We tend to think of our ancestors as being decisive and acting in concert for a common cause, and maybe they were, in civilized places like Portsmouth or Boston.

But Raymond?

According to Fullonton, town meetings, in the first few years of incorporation, were held at the Bean Tavern, which, at first, was simply the home of Lieutenant Benjamin Bean. We assume that rum was available.

In January 1768, it was voted to build a meetinghouse, away from the rum, on what is now Batchelder Road, about a mile westerly of Old Fremont Road. Two months later, an attempt was made to revoke that vote, which failed. But the next month, a prevailing vote moved the preferred site to a place between the tavern and the pound, which was a little north of the tavern—that is, closer to the rum.

In September, some folks living in the Lane district tried to revoke this location and failed. Then they attempted to rejoin their part of town to Chester, and that failed.

Apparently, the new site between the pound and the tavern was not acceptable to a sufficient number, for the next year, a petition was sent to the provincial assembly for help in relocating the meetinghouse. The assembly advised putting it back on Batchelder Road, but more westerly and farther from the rum. The town accepted, and someone ordered timber to be drawn to the site.

At the 1770 town meeting (at the tavern), an article was offered to appoint a committee to build the meetinghouse. The article failed.

At the 1771 meeting (at the tavern), a committee was formed to "take care" of the timber left at the Batchelder Road site.

In 1773, "it was determined to have a meetinghouse." Perhaps to satisfy everyone, it was decided to place it at the geographical center of town, which turned out to be in the middle of the river. Then, after two votes, Pitch Pine Plain on the easterly side of "Freetown Pond" (now Lake Carroll) was chosen. Pitch Pine Plain, according to Fullonton, is where the Common is located. The next year, on June 6, 1774, all previous votes were revoked as to the meetinghouse site, and it was instead decided to place it more easterly, probably what is now mid–Epping Street.

"The raising" of the frame "was a great affair." Rum was provided.

In 1775, a vote was held to move the frame. The vote failed. The Revolution began, and ten years elapsed.

At the meeting of 1785, it was voted to build the meetinghouse. The previously built frame had been used to build the Pecker Bridge. The new location was on Cider Ferry Road, located approximately behind what is now the safety complex. On June 14, 1786, the new structure was raised. One of the selectmen was paid to furnish a barrel of rum.

In 1788, the meetinghouse was completed to the extent that a meeting was held there. We're not sure what time the meeting started, but we know that it quickly adjourned to take up most of the business at the tavern.

Two years later, in 1790, another attempt was made to have the town meeting at the meetinghouse. It was adjourned to a later date, at the tavern.

In 1793, glass had been installed at the meetinghouse. One is inclined to wonder if there was a reason for this tardiness in making a meeting place weather tight.

In 1797, the meetinghouse was still not quite in the right place. Although it was near the center of town, it was not near the center of business—that is, the village. On May 22, it was voted to move the building again.

There were at least six votes for moving, for raising the money and whether to revoke either throughout the summer until a final vote in October.

Plans were made for the moving. Those against it prayed for divine intervention. Fullonton writes that there were *80 pairs* (my emphasis) of oxen assembled to drag the building. I find it hard to imagine 160 members of the bovine ilk arranged two by two along the road. At ten feet per pair, the oxen would have stretched some eight hundred feet, or over a tenth of a mile. The fertilizer that was produced must have been a wondrous sight and fragrance.

General Joseph Cilley, he of the recent Revolutionary War, was in charge. The Reverend Peter Holt, from Epping, offered prayer.

During the moving, one of the carrying-stringers broke, and some celebrated with their own prayers. I assume that others went to the tavern.

Some went to the woods to cut new stringers, and the next day, it is said, there were more oxen, *one hundred twenty pairs*![*]

By sundown that day, the deed was done, and the meetinghouse was in the position that it occupied for the next 120 years.

So it took from 1768 to 1797, dozens of votes and doubtless hundreds of prayers to settle the location of the meetinghouse. There is no record of the amount of rum that was consumed.

*I have wondered how 240 oxen were assembled. The number suggests that almost everyone had at least one ox. Being born a male calf likely meant castration at an early age and a lifetime of burden, only to end up in the stew. The only other options were to be veal or, if lucky, to be kept to service the heifers, which would be OK for awhile, but ultimately they would still end up in the stew.

Retrospective

Historian Joseph Fullonton was a confirmed teetotaler. In his account of the first raising of the frame, he offers a poem:

A church to raise in Raymond town;
A crowd comes there from miles around,—
Old men, young men and barefoot boys;
The frame is large, a host employs.

The broadsides man, the breadth and length;
Our fathers were of giant strength;
Up, up, the sides go, firm they stand,
The promise is a building grand.

Bring on the girts, the braces, beams,
Boys, throw aloft the fastening pins;
The rafters next and purlins long,
The ridge-pole last;—the frame is strong.

A barrel of New England rum
Was furnished by the Selectmen;
All drank three times, the story's great,
I s'pose 'twas for "the stomach's sake."

Since then the truth has worked "like leaven";
Reform has come, thank gracious Heaven;—
Let all respect themselves and shun
The "liquid fire," the tippler's doom.

Speaking only for myself, of course, some of the selectmen's meetings I sat through would have been much more tolerable with a cold beer and munchies at hand. I'm not much for rum.

But the final history of Raymond's town hall is yet to be written. The original "permanent" town hall, or meetinghouse, burned in 1917. Its foundation stood there for many years between the fire station and the library. And behind the foundation, in what had been the cellar of the meetinghouse, was a jail of sorts—a cage of steel bars, which is now situated at the historical society.

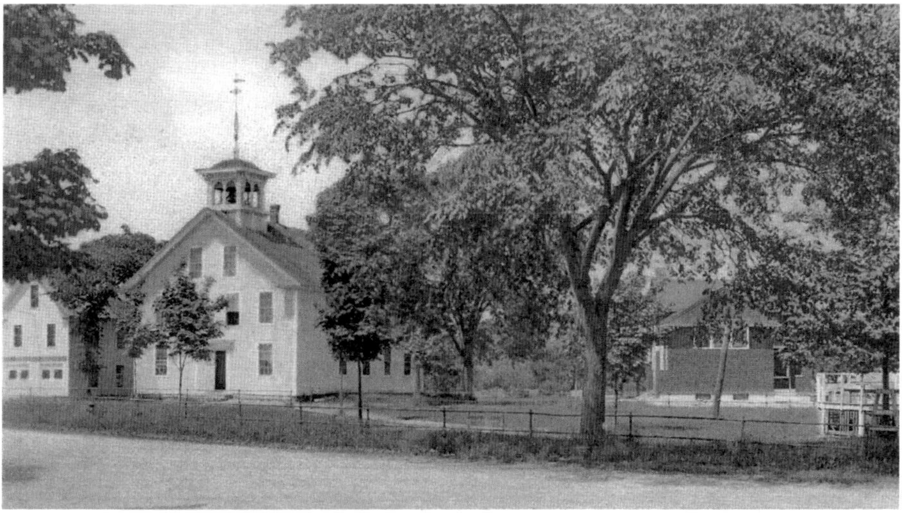

Original meetinghouse (right), fire station (left). The meetinghouse was built in the late 1700s and the fire station in the early 1900s. *Courtesy of Joyce Wood's postcard collection.*

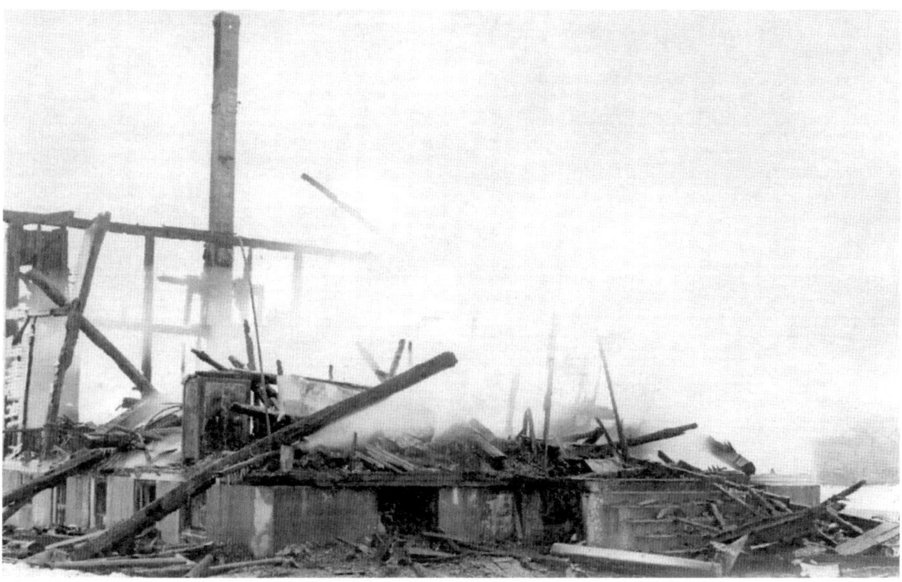

Remains of the original meetinghouse, 1917. *Courtesy of Joyce Wood's postcard collection.*

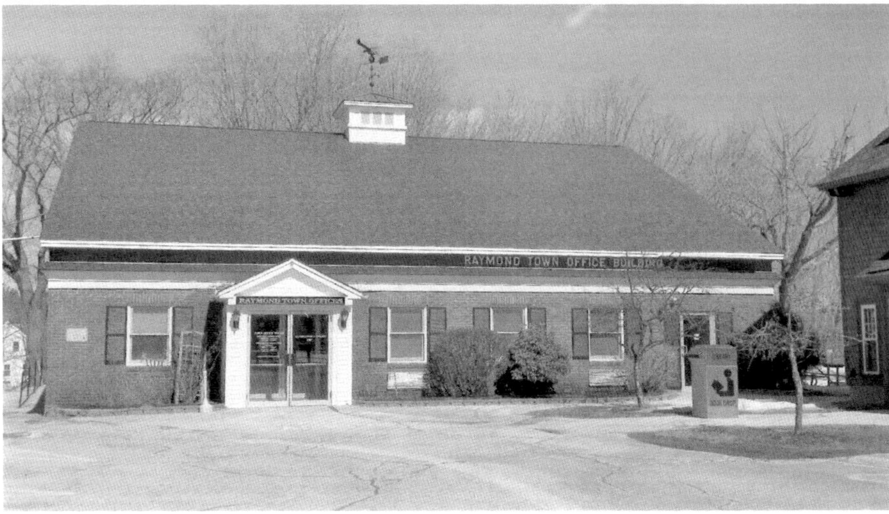

Raymond Town Office Building. *Courtesy of Paul Brown.*

In the early '70s, after considerable debate, the present town office was built. I have always felt some bemusement at the letters on the front of the building—"RAYMOND TOWN OFFICE BUILDING"—as if it weren't perfectly obvious that it is a building.

12

COMMUNITY ORGANIZATIONS

Hurd-Welch Post #90 of the American Legion

By Harold Wood

Raymond Post #90 of the American Legion received its charter in 1946. Although records are nonexistent, the post apparently flourished for a number of years, but the membership numbers dwindled until, in the early 1990s, the membership was down to about fifteen members.

In the 1990s, then post commander Richard "Rick" Smith and Edward "Tompy" Thompson would go door to door to collect the dues for the new year. The post was a post on paper only.

In early 2003, Edward Martini called many of the veterans on the mailing list and decided that the veterans in town would like to have American Legion meetings. Through his efforts, the Post started meetings in April of that year in the Veterans of Foreign Wars (VFW) meeting room. At that first meeting, a slate of officers was elected, with Ed Martini elected as post commander.

In May 2003, the post voted to name the post Hurd-Welch Post #90, recognizing the dedication and service of Ted Welch and Palmer T. Hurd, both local veterans.

The post continued to meet in the VFW meeting room until early 2012, when members voted to find their own post home. The American Legion had never had a building solely theirs, having always met in any convenient location. A contract was executed with Edward and Arlene Jewett to lease a portion of the building at the corner of Harriman Hill Road and Route 27 in July of that year and renovations of the designated space started immediately, with many volunteers contributing numerous hours to convert the space from a hair salon and spa into the current American Legion Post.

The Legion home was basically completed and was occupied in February 2013. The post has its own canteen and has been very active with bingo and other fundraising activities. The membership numbers continue to increase, and the building is now home to Hurd-Welch Post #90 of the American Legion, the Post #90 Auxiliary, the Post #90 Sons of the American Legion and Chapter #90 of the American Legion Riders, a very successful motorcycle club.

Some of the recent commanders were as follows:

2003–2005: Edward Martini
2005–2010: David Peno
2010–2011: Paul Clements
2011–2013: Warren Black
2013–2014: Christopher Derzanski

Hurd-Welch American Legion Post #90 was named in honor of Palmer T. Hurd, son of Mary and William Hurd (longtime Raymond druggist), and Frederick (Ted) Welch. Hurd was a member of the class of 1942 at RHS and answered his nation's call, serving in the U.S. Marine Corps as a runner at Guadalcanal in the Pacific Theater, earning him the U.S. Navy's Bronze Star Medal for "heroic achievement while serving with the Third Marine Division during action against enemy Japanese forces" in September 1943. Welch, a lifelong resident of Raymond, was commander of the American Legion Post #90 for several years, veteran of the U.S. Army during the Korean Conflict and past member of Maple-Wheadon VFW Post #4479.

Boy Scouts of America in Raymond

By Anthony Dickerson (Life Scout, Troop 3)

Troop 100 was the first Boy Scout troop in Raymond; it was chartered in 1939 by the Raymond Parent-Teacher Association. Henry Hastings was the troop's first Scoutmaster. In 1942, Hughin Holt and Robert Cammett were the first Scouts in Raymond to achieve Eagle Scout, the highest rank in Boy Scouts. Both Holt and Cammett were chosen as pages for the International Monetary Conference of 1944, held in the White Mountains. Although both were chosen, only Holt could attend. Troop 100 remained solid until the mid-1950s, when it lost momentum and dissolved in 1958.

In 1962, Troop 100 was reestablished. The troop was sponsored by Regis Tanning Company. Donald Morin became scoutmaster. Other Troop 100 sponsors have been the Lions Club, Raymond United Methodist Church, Congregational Church of Raymond, Raymond Sportsman's Club, and Raymond Firefighter's Association. Troop 100 became known for its high adventure activities, especially for its canoeing and backpacking trips.

A second Boy Scout troop, Troop 111, was chartered on December 1, 1991, by the Raymond Volunteer Fireman's Association. Earl Lavoie was Troop 111's first scoutmaster. The troop offered a different program than that offered by Troop 100. Troop 111 began to wane, and Kevin Woods was asked to become scoutmaster. Troop 111 reformed under his leadership in 1996. Troop 111's fundraisers included a food stand in Portsmouth's New Year celebrations and an annual craft fair, which Troop 101 still runs. From 2001 to 2005, Troop 111 had fifteen boys achieve the rank of Eagle Scout.

Troops 100 and 111 continued to serve the town for many years. In 2010, the two troops merged, forming Troop 101. The troop number was chosen as a compromise between Troops 100 and 111, as one digit from each troop was taken. The number also recognizes the main artery through Raymond, Route 101. The troop sponsor is the Raymond Firefighter's Association, with secondary sponsorship by the Raymond Sportsman's Club. Marc Zahler was the first scoutmaster of newly formed Troop 101.

Troop 3 was chartered on February 1, 2011, by the Congregational Church of Raymond. Jonathan McCosh Sr. became the first scoutmaster of Troop 3. The troop number was selected to represent the three parts of the Scout Oath.

Cub Scout Pack 100 was founded in 1971. Stewart Belden was the first cubmaster. The pack was sponsored by the Raymond United Methodist

Church. In the 1970s, membership in Pack 100 slowly dwindled; however, it was saved by some concerned Raymondites. The pack once again became successful and had over one hundred Cub Scouts by the 1980s. Past sponsors include the Congregational Church of Raymond, Raymond Firefighter's Association and Hurd-Welch Post #90 of the American Legion.

The Tiger Cub program in Raymond was started in the 1980s and was separate from the Cub Scouts. In 2001, Boy Scouts of America announced that the Tiger program would become part of Cub Scouts of America.

Beginning in 1930, Camp Onway provided summer camp activities for Scouts from Massachusetts and for local Scouts. Camp Onway began as a YMCA camp in the early 1900s and ran through the 1929 season. In 2007, Camp Onway was sold to the Church of Jesus Christ of Latter-day Saints and is now a summer camp for Mormon girls under the new name of Zion's Camp. Local Scouting troops and packs and the historic district continue to use this camp during the off-season months for camping and other Scouting activities.

From 1942 through 2013, sixty Raymond Boy Scouts have achieved the rank of Eagle Scout. Some Eagle Scout service projects throughout Raymond have included the Raymond Fire Department Smokey Bear fire sign, historic markers around town, Dearborn Forest kiosk and trail markers, Raymond Baptist Church prayer garden, Riverside Park Eagle Trail, Riverside Park exercise stations and the Cable Committee walkway.

As of 2013, over ninety youth are served by Scouting programs in Raymond, which include Cub Scout Pack 100, Boy Scout Troops 3 and 101, Police Explorer Post 485 and Fire Explorer Post 100. You may meet these Scouts selling frappés, pancakes, popcorn, wreaths or nuts. You may also talk to them at silent auctions, spaghetti dinners or craft fairs. You may see them parking vehicles, collecting food for local pantries, placing American flags at veterans' grave stones, marching in town parades, saluting at 9/11 memorials and providing general town cleanup and services to the community of Raymond.

As Raymond, New Hampshire, celebrates 250 years, Scouting has fulfilled its seventy-fifth year of service in Raymond by preparing young people to make ethical and moral choices throughout their lives in accordance with the Scout Oath and Law.

Raymond Area Rotary Club

By Tim Louis

Rotary is an organization of business and professional persons united worldwide who provide humanitarian service, encourage high ethical standards in all vocations and help build goodwill and peace in the world.

The Raymond Area Rotary Club serves the communities of Candia, Deerfield, Epping, Fremont, Nottingham and Raymond. The club meets every Wednesday from 7:30 to 8:30 a.m. at the Ray-Fre Senior Citizens Center, 64 Main Street, Raymond. At each meeting, members socialize, conduct a brief meeting, enjoy a breakfast prepared by the seniors and conclude with a twenty- to thirty-minute presentation from a guest speaker.

During the winter of 1990, a group of businessmen and women led by Dr. Paul Silver, a local dentist, gathered in a meeting room of the Raymond Congregational Church to plan the formation of a Rotary Club. As plans progressed, they decided to include the towns of Raymond, Fremont, Epping, Deerfield and Nottingham, and thus the Raymond Area Rotary Club was born.

The club was sponsored by the Exeter Rotary Club and was chartered in June 1990 with a total membership of forty-one. As was Rotary policy at the time, one had only to live or work in the community that the club represented in order to become a member.

The initial Raymond members were Barbara Beardsley, Reginald Maisey, Ray Saulnier, Jim Fortin, Tim Louis, John Cole, Peter Lindahl, Martha St. Amand, Dr. Paul Silver, Inez Welch, Neal Welch, Karen Tenney, Catherine Del Tufo, Tony Santilli, Dick Dolan and Neil Iverson.

The Raymond Area Rotary Club was admitted to Rotary International on June 10, 1990.

The club has provided annual college scholarships for students in the communities served, sponsored blood drives, conducted town and highway cleanups and provided fifty holiday food baskets for the needy at both Thanksgiving and Christmas. Raymond Rotary was the primary initiator and sponsor of the Raymond High School chemical-free graduation party twenty-three years ago.

Raymond Rotary also supplied thermal imaging cameras for the Raymond and Deerfield Fire Departments and most recently helped fund an Automated External Defibrillator (AED) for the Ray-Fre Center for use by the seniors if the occasion should arise. It has supported local parks and conservation areas, partnered with foreign clubs to deliver hundreds of wheelchairs to Haiti and Jamaica, sent a container of medical equipment and supplies to Nigeria and financed freshwater wells in Africa. The club has been active with Rotary International in Central America, building schools and clinics and providing low-cost water filtration systems to remote villages. It has joined clubs all over the world in campaigns for literacy, environmental awareness and cultural exchange. Most notably, it has nearly attained its goal set over five years ago to eradicate polio from the planet. As signified by its motto "Service Above Self," Rotary's main objective is service: in the community, in the workplace and throughout the world.

Greater Raymond Chamber of Commerce

By David Howard

In the early 1990s, business owners who were volunteering on various town committees were being asked what the "business community" thought about certain matters in town. Local CPA Dave Howard realized that there really wasn't an organization in town that could be representative or a voice of the business community.

In those pre-Internet and e-mail days, using the Yellow Pages to compile a list, a mailer was sent to businesses in town to see if there was an interest in such an organization. On October 12, 1994, the first meeting of the Raymond Business Owners was held, and it was clear from the attendance that there was an interest in forming an organization.

On January 18, 1995, a second meeting was held and representatives from the Barrington and Northwood Chambers of Commerce were invited to speak about their respective chambers and to answer questions.

On February 8, 1995, an organizational meeting was held, and the Raymond Chamber of Commerce was officially formed. On May 10, 1995, the organization voted to change its name to the Greater Raymond Chamber of Commerce. By June 30, 1995, the chamber had reached its goal of seventy-five chartered members. By November 8, 1995, the chamber had ninety-seven members.

The chamber has been active in town activities over the years, holding an annual Business Expo, sponsoring the town's annual Halloween Party and participating in the town fair and July 4 parade. In 1997, the chamber raised over $30,000 toward the building of a playground off Route 107. The chamber hosts various "Business after Hours" meetings and quarterly business meetings and awards an annual "Business of the Year" award.

The Greater Raymond Chamber of Commerce's mission is to develop a positive and productive business climate in the town of Raymond. The primary responsibilities of the chamber are to serve as an advocate for the promotion of business and community development and to communicate the views of the business community.

Almost twenty years later, the chamber still holds to the above mission statement and continues to be a resource for Raymond-area businesses. Visit the Greater Raymond Chamber of Commerce at www.raymondareachamberofcommerce.com, or contact the chamber at info@raymondareachamber.com.

Raymond Coalition for Youth

By Celeste Menard

The Raymond Coalition for Youth was established as a nonprofit organization on January 24, 2004, to promote positive healthy choices for youth. Its mission is to empower the community to promote positive youth development and strengthen community assets by coordinating services and opportunities through prevention initiatives, including those directed at suicide, alcohol, tobacco and other drugs.

The coalition is made up of many volunteers, but five founding members—Michael Chouinard, Julie Hazell-Felch, Kelly Lehman, police chief David Salois and Stephen Sloan—put their names on the official paperwork.

In 2001, the University of New Hampshire assembled a group of people who cared about Raymond and its youth to look at results from a Youth Risk Behavior Survey. At that time, Raymond's rate of alcohol, tobacco and other drug use was very high as compared with the state's.

The coalition works with the Town of Raymond but is financially independent through the support of grants and donations that are used to directly support its mission and local youth. Raymond Coalition for Youth Action includes young people in Raymond who voice their concerns and act to create positive change. They are the driving force of the group's mission and goals.

The following lists Raymond Coalition for Youth's impact over the past ten years:

- Youth Risk Behavior Survey results show that reported use of alcohol, tobacco and other drugs has dramatically fallen.
- Over six hundred people have been trained in suicide prevention.
- After-school programming keeps youth safe during after-school hours.
- Hundreds of youth have been members of Raymond Coalition for Youth Action, empowered to have a voice and make a difference for their peers and the community.
- Educational programming and prevention messaging efforts, such as Project Safeguard, Family Fun Night, Operation Raymond Clean Up, Sticker Shock and Red Ribbon Week, have gone state- and nationwide.
- A family playground at Riverside Park has been built.

Ray-Fre Senior Citizen's Club, Inc.

By Gladys Brunelle, with Carol Reed

In 1968, a group of seniors met at the Fremont Methodist Church and later met in Raymond at the United Methodist Church. These two groups decided to join together as membership grew.

The need for a permanent place was discussed, and a committee was appointed to find one. Robert Clement Real Estate was contacted and informed the committee that the old A&P store on Main Street was available. After many meetings and discussions, the membership voted to buy the property in 1972 for $29,000, at a monthly rate of $275 for a twelve-year period.

After buying the building, moving in for the first meeting was a challenge. The only furniture was donated by members. Each member donated five dollars to buy folding chairs. Legs were bought for tables, and plywood was purchased to make tabletops. Kitchen cabinets were donated, as were dishes that were being discarded from the Brentwood Nursing Home. Donations of furniture, a piano and U.S. and New Hampshire flags were received.

A nearby restaurant was going out of business, and the owner stated that he would donate bins of dishes, pots and pans, glassware, coffee thermoses and silverware to the club.

In January 1973, a meeting to form a corporation was held. The Articles of Agreement were drawn up and signed by the incorporators. In accordance with the Articles of Agreement, the club, now known as Ray-Fre Senior Citizen's Club, Inc., met at 1:30 p.m. to vote on accepting the bylaws. At that time, bylaws and rules and regulations followed. Also at that time, the club became officially chartered in Concord on January 17, 1973.

Today, Ray-Fre is in the twenty-first century. The club has three computers, and scheduled activities consist of billiards, bingo, cribbage, line dancing, walking, exercise programs, knitting and crocheting, sitting and chatting, bridge, whist, monthly specials and Meals on Wheels.

The club supports itself by July and Christmas fairs and the sale of donated items.

The center is open to the public every day except Sunday. To be eligible to participate in any activity, one has to be fifty years of age and a member of the club.

Raymond Historical Society

By Diane White

When the Raymond Historical Society celebrated its twenty-fifth anniversary in September 1995, members Shirley Barnes, Sue Ege, A. Willis Goddard, Iber Holmes Gove, Mildred and George Guptill, Ruth Hoffman, Thelma Holt, Caroline and Arthur Severance and Dorothy Tilton, some of the society's founding members, were among the celebrants. In 2009, the society celebrated its fortieth anniversary with far fewer of its founding members but with many more town members thanks to a membership drive spearheaded by Diane Debruyckere over a one-year period. The membership drive was in response to the Finley Challenge (2008), whose goal was to engage people in saving and sharing history. The drive gave automatic membership to all the schoolchildren of Raymond and provided family memberships to many of the citizens of Raymond as well. The need for members continues to this day because although the founding fathers were diligent in their mission to "Preserve the Past," they were less instructive in how we would "Prepare the Future." As a result, this private, nonprofit, totally volunteer organization continues to struggle with finances.

The society's home is the former 1892 railroad depot, purchased in 1973 from Pearl Guptill Eccleston. The building was placed on the National Register of Historic Places in 1979, the same year the mortgage was paid off. Over the years, the society acquired the World War II Civil Defense Building, the Candia Wait Station, the Boston & Main Section Car House, the Gile School, one of nine one-room schoolhouses of Raymond and a number of "rolling stock" items, including a Whitcomb engine, a caboose, an inspection car and a refrigerated boxcar.

The section house holds the museum of early tools and farm memorabilia established by member Stephen Goldthwaite. Raymond's first ladder wagon (used at fires) is also stored there and is still in need of repair. The Gile School, moved to its present site in 1981, is equipped with early classroom furniture, complete with a wood stove, kerosene lamps and other schoolhouse memorabilia. It appears as it did at the turn of the century and continues to be a source of interest for schoolchildren tours. Funds for the care and upkeep of this schoolhouse, once located in the Scribner Road area of town, were left to the society by Edith Hammond, whose contributions were many and varied over the years as a longtime member of the society. Were it not for Edith, the first roof replacement on the depot in 2003 could not have been completed. Additionally, the society continues to provide a Raymond High School graduating senior with a scholarship from the Gile School through the efforts of Betty Goldthwaite, a Hammond descendant.

The society was provided oversight of the original Boston Post Cane and has facilitated the awarding of the cane over the years to Raymond's oldest citizens. Barney Shaffer was the first to receive the cane in 1987 following the renewal of this town tradition. Grover Moulton was awarded the cane in the early '80s. Other verified cane holders include Mildred Hall in 2001, Mabel Morrison in July 2003, Caroline Severance in December 2003 and Edith Higgins in May 2008. Its present holder is Eldon "Bob" McKinley, who received the cane in November 2012 at a ceremony held in Torrent Hall.

In 2002, the society began an ongoing fundraising project of establishing a memorial walkway, with pavers purchased by friends and families and inscribed with memorials to loved ones. These are still available today. Later, a map and walking tour narrative guide of the historical sites in Raymond's downtown area was published. This was developed in 2012 by members Fritz Bell and Will Fregosi and continues to have additions.

Abigail's Attic Sale during the annual town fair, the August Pancake Breakfast sponsored by Walmart and the Holly Fair at Christmas after the Tree Lighting on the Common continue to be the society's major fundraising activities. Open house is held at the depot and Gile School following the town Tree Lighting and Christmas Parade with hot cocoa and cookies furnished by society members and the town recreation department. There are only a few times a year when all buildings on the Raymond Historical Society's property are open to the public and manned by members with knowledge of the historical significance of each building. These are events worth attending.

In 2010, Pelmac Industries was contracted to provide ongoing security surveillance of the entire RHS property, with the assistance of the Raymond Police Department, a service that continues today. Additionally, to meet the needs of the elderly and handicapped, the society can now provide a pictorial view of its buildings and rolling stock through picture books produced by Walgreen's and available at the depot.

In 2013, fundraising began for the refurbishment of the 1892 depot, beginning with the replacement of a second new roof completed in December 2013. Further work on the exterior painting, and window refurbishment, will commence in the spring of 2014. Additional work, including repair and restoration of the rolling stock, will proceed as funds become available.

Present officers are Diane White, president; Diane DeBruyckere, vice-president; Joyce M. D. Wood, secretary; Marjorie Desjardins, treasurer.

Raymond Voter Information Project

By Carolyn Matthews

The Raymond Voter Information Project (Raymond VIP) was conceived in May 2009, when four Raymond residents, Gretchen Gott, Cheryl Killam, Carolyn Matthews and Joyce Wood, met over lunch to discuss Raymond's loss of its primary newspaper and the lack of information for local elections.

An exploratory committee formed and met through the summer to establish core values and founding principles for Articles of Agreement, filed with the state on September 21, 2009 and codified into bylaws approved on January 12, 2010. On July 6, 2011, the Raymond Voter Information Project was recognized as a New Hampshire Charitable Trust, and on July 25, 2012, it received official recognition as an IRS 501(c)(3) organization, retroactive to September 21, 2009. This designation helped Raymond VIP obtain a grant for strategic planning from the New Hampshire Charitable Foundation in September 2012.

Founding members are Sherry Brox, Barbara Edgar, Marilyn Elliott, Sandra Ellis, Gretchen Gott, Linda Hoelzel, Kathy Lee, Carolyn Matthews, Kathy Mayo, Leslie O'Donnell, Sally Paradis, Jeannie Richards, Marilyn Semple, Kim Tyndall, Colleen West-Coates, Joyce Wood, Traci York and Dana Zulager.

The object of the Raymond Voter Information Project is the advancement of education to enable students and community members to prepare to exercise their civil right to vote with the greatest freedom of choice.

To meet this objective, to date Raymond VIP has produced five annual voting guides for local elections using a three-tiered editorial process: reporters gather information on both sides of issues, citizen readers review and an Editorial Committee ensures that that all analyses are clear, comprehensive and objective. The guide began as an insert in the *CarriageTowne News* and is now mailed to every household in Raymond.

Raymond VIP began sponsoring a middle school writing challenge in 2010. Winning essays appear in the voting guide to inspire participation in the election process. Essays by Alyssa Mae White and Andrew Meade (2010), Cameron Rowton (2011), Alyssa Sylvia and Colton Corriveau (2012) and Noah Kierstead and Morgan Murray (2013) are available at www.raymondvip.org. The Raymond VIP Fall Speaker Program has brought to Raymond Benjamin Frost, Esq., ("How to Write a Citizen's Petition Warrant Article"); Dr. Vanessa Druskat of the University of New Hampshire ("Your Most Important Role in a Democracy: Thinking for Yourself"); Raymond town moderator Kathleen Hoelzel ("The New Voter Identification Laws"); and Dr. Andrew Smith of the UNH Survey Center ("A Profile of Today's Voter"). Programs are telecast on RCTV and used in school classrooms.

For more information, visit www.raymondvip.org.

Raymond High School Alumni Association

By Sally Paradis

The first RHS Alumni Association was formed in 1932 at a meeting held at the Pilgrim Inn. The tradition of holding annual alumni banquets and awarding a scholarship at graduation continued through the mid-'60s, when the association disbanded due to a lack of interest. Successful reunions, however, were held during the town's celebrations in 1964 and in 1989.

With the twenty-first century approaching, a group of "Raymondites" planned an all-class reunion that holds the record for attendees with nearly seven hundred alumni, guests and former staff members from all over the country gathering at the new RHS on July 9, 2000. In honor of the occasion, a video production titled *RHS Through the Years* was produced, honoring the school's proud tradition and eighty-two-year history. It is available at the Raymond Historical Society, Dudley-Tucker Library and RHS library.

The success of the event provided the impetus for the committee to continue. Bylaws were adopted, and officers elected: president, Sally Guptill Paradis, '58; vice-president, Andrew Maloney, '66; secretaries Shirley Holt Dodge, '49, and Charlena Littlefield Thompson ,'44; and treasurer, Barbara Gosselin Porter, '51. Directors included Edna (Severance) and Paul Berry, '47; Elayne Ingalls Clark, '65; Mary Hrycuna Hayes, '65; Romeo Levesque Jr., '55; and Chris Mataragas, '67.

Homecoming 2005 bid "farewell" to Raymond Consolidated School, which had served the community since 1918. David Baker, '51, presented the history of the school, from the one-room schoolhouses to the fire that destroyed the town hall, creating the need for the "consolidated" school in 1917. The newly instituted RHS Athletic Hall of Fame was introduced by athletic director Davinney Brazeau. In closing, Principal Emeritus John Callaghan called on the community members to "continue their tradition of helping one another as they had done for years so that greater benefit for all could be realized," followed by his rendering of the "Irish Blessing."

Homecoming 2010 saw three hundred alumni and friends at the Iber Holmes Gove Middle School. Former principal John Callaghan was honored with an alumni-produced DVD, *John Callaghan: Educator, Coach, Citizen, Family Man*. Tribute was also paid to former beloved teacher and coach Cynthia Lord, and a collection of notes written by former students, colleagues and friends was presented to her.

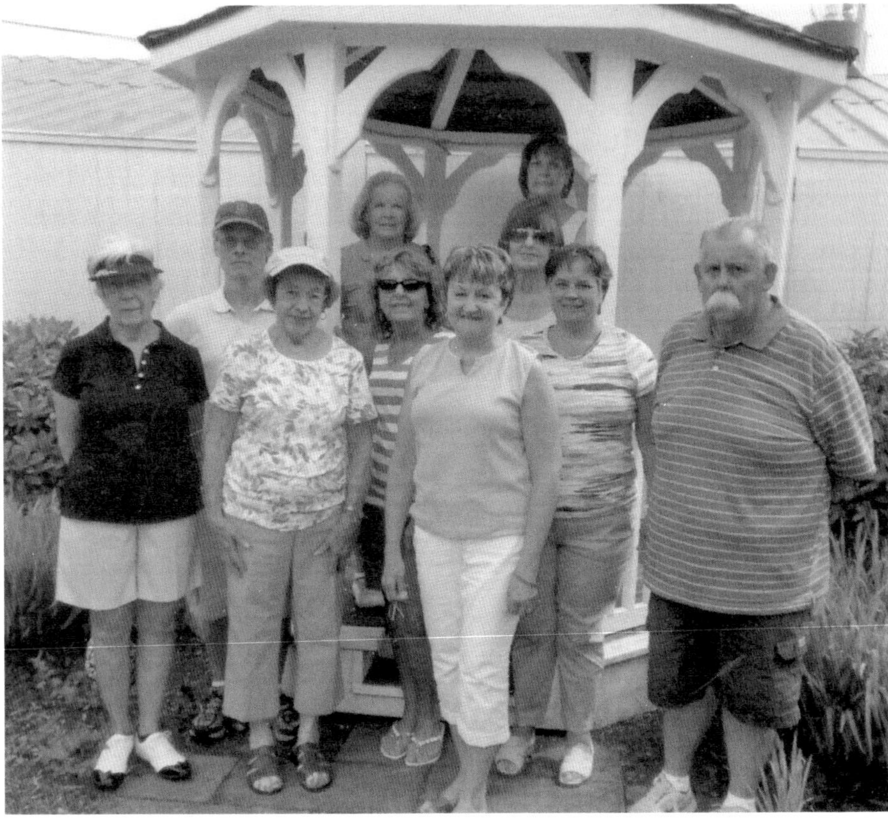

2013 Alumni committee. Front row (from left): Sally Paradis, Barbara Porter, Elayne Ingalls, Chris Mataragas. Row two: Michael Foley, Terrie Dolan, Carol Levesque. Row three: Shirley Dodge, Judy Foley. Back row: Cathy Del Tufo. *Courtesy of Sally Paradis.*

On November 2, 2012, members of the association presented a plaque to the Iber Holmes Gove Middle School in memory of Cynthia Lord for her many years of outstanding service and to perpetuate her legacy in the hearts and minds of thousands of students and colleagues whose lives she touched.

The awarding of scholarships continues as a primary purpose of the association, and since 2000, $88,000 has been awarded to deserving seniors of RHS. These funds have been raised with an annual golf outing held at Candia Woods each year through the generosity of area businesses, organizations, class, family, memorial sponsorships and the participants.

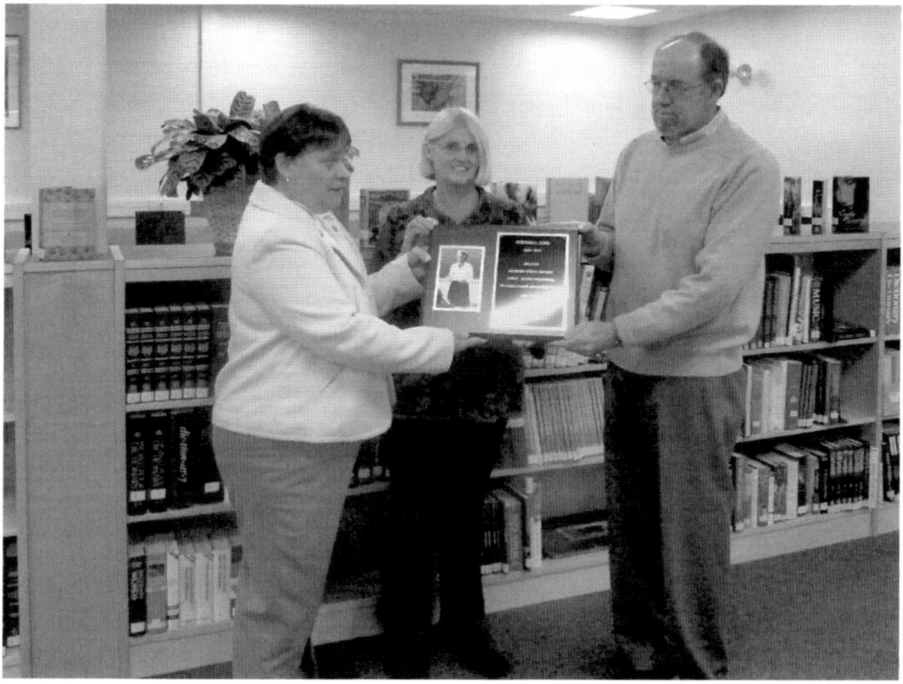

From left: Carol Levesque, president of RHS Alumni Association; Ellen Small, principal of IHGMS; and Robert Lord '74, son of Cynthia L. Lord, at the Cynthia L. Lord Memorial Plaque presentation, November 2, 2012. *Courtesy of Sally Paradis.*

In October 2012, Cathy Perkins Del Tufo, '74, and Terrie Brackett Dolan, '74, were elected vice-president and treasurer, respectively. Michael Foley, '68, replaced longtime board member Annette Quintal, '47, and Carol Martin Levesque, '70, also joined by virtue of her being past president. Barbara Gosselin Porter, '51, received a vote of thanks for ten years of dedicated service as treasurer. In February 2014, the committee was saddened by the passing of thirteen-year committee and board member Romeo Levesque Jr., '55. Andrew Maloney, '66, was appointed to fill Romeo's unexpired term. An all-class reunion will be held during the 250th celebration in September.

Raymond Riverside Park

By Pamela Turcotte

Riverside Park was a dream of Henry Turcotte, who wanted a place for the community to go to enjoy nature—a people's park is what he called it. It started in 1997, when the town swapped a 1.6-acre building lot with Henry for 16.0 acres located along the Lamprey River. In 2001, the voters supported the purchase of over 44.0 acres adjacent to the 16.0 acres, and Raymond Riverside Park was born. In 1998, Sally Paradis and George Guptill Jr. donated 1.0 acre along Route 27 and the Lamprey River to be included as part of Riverside Park in memory of their grandfather Dr. George H. Guptill. The Riverside Park Committee was developed in 1998, when a nonprofit entity was formed whose purpose was to raise funds for improvements and promote the use of the park so the community members could have a clean, healthy place to bring their families.

In 2003, improvements started on the land and included grading and beautifying by Aggregate Industries, Timberland, Boy Scout Troop 100, Raymond Area Rotary Club, Bemis Construction, Scenic Nursery, the Town of Raymond and many other community members. Over the years, many individuals and businesses have given their time and money to make the park what it is today: a hidden jewel in the heart of Raymond. The park features a memorial garden, a dog park known as Riverside Bark, horseshoe pits, hiking trails, fishing along the Lamprey, picnic tables, a stage and an open field used for functions such as the Earth Day Celebration, a winter carnival, musical festivals and Arts in the Park.

The park received a big facelift this year when the committee partnered with the Raymond Coalition for Youth (www.rcfy.org) to install playground equipment. With grants from Lowe's and Walmart procured by the coalition, the equipment was purchased, but the site work still had to be done. Aggregate Industries, along with Bemis Construction, Lisa Hutchinson of Dirt Shapes and many community members, came together to clear trails and brush and get the site ready for the playground equipment. Aggregate installed all the equipment as a community service project, and Lisa Hutchinson and Bemis Construction did the final site work. The playground was dedicated in a small ceremony in September 2012.

Visit the park on Facebook or e-mail it at RaymondRiverside@gmail.com.

Reach High Scholars Program

By John McDaniels

Reach High Scholars Program (RHSP) encourages Raymond students to "reach high" in pursuit of their education. It provides initiatives at no cost to the school district that are unique for a community like Raymond. RHSP was started in 2007 by a group of RHS alumni, faculty, parents and members of the community under the leadership of John McDaniels (RHS '52). It is an independent New Hampshire nonprofit corporation and a tax-exempt organization under section 501(c)(3) of the Internal Revenue Code. A full description of RHSP and its activities are on its website: www.reachhighscholars.org.

RHSP provides a continuum of initiatives that starts after the seventh grade with three successive summers of Raymond Roundtables, an academic enrichment program conducted in Raymond by Phillips Exeter Academy. In their sophomore year, students become active in the Reach High Scholars Club, a student extracurricular activity, and do a PSAT prep course. After their sophomore and junior years, all students are encouraged to attend summer boarding enrichment programs, at Phillips Exeter, Brown University and St. Paul's School. While juniors, the students attend college fairs, visit colleges, complete a PSAT/SAT prep course of fourteen sessions (conducted at RHS by Academic Approach, a nationally recognized organization) and take the SAT twice.

RHSP was instrumental in having RHS selected in 2010 to participate in the Summer Enrichment at Dartmouth (SEAD) program. SEAD expands the educational opportunities for promising high school students from selected under-resourced urban and rural schools. SEAD selects students for the program who have the potential and desire to achieve excellence but may have lacked the resources and support systems necessary to succeed. They want students showing high promise rather than those with high achievement. SEAD provides the guidance to help these students expand their educational options and opportunities.

RHS is now one of four high schools in the country in the SEAD program. Eight current RHS sophomores are at Dartmouth each summer for two or three weeks during their four high school years. In addition, there are three Dartmouth students at RHS and living in Raymond for successive nine-week periods each year to mentor the RHS SEAD students and to promote college awareness in RHS.

The introduction of these initiatives by RHSP has had a dramatic impact on college acceptances by RHS students. In Raymond's 244-year history through 2008, eighteen RHS students are known to have graduated from one of a list of ninety highly competitive colleges. The list of those colleges and the names of the RHS alumni who graduated from them over the years are on RHSP's website. (Please notify RHSP of anyone who was overlooked. Additional role models for the current students are always welcomed.)

That 244-year record has been broken by the classes of '09–'13, with nineteen students who went to those colleges. Most of them have financial aid with small amounts of debt and need-based grants of up to $50,000 per annum that, over four years, will have a total value of about $2 million. A list with the colleges and students' names is on RHSP's website.

The RHS classes of 2011–2013 have sent 6.5 percent of their graduates to highly competitive colleges. None of the other high schools in southeastern New Hampshire (Dover, Exeter, Oyster River, Portsmouth, St. Thomas Aquinas, Spaulding, Winnacunnet) has sent more than 3 percent.

Tucker Lodge #99, F&AM

By Clarence Robbins and John Steward

On May 18, 1904, thirty-two master Masons sent a petition to Grand Lodge Meeting asking for the creation of a new Lodge in Raymond through dispensation. The grand master at the time (J. Henry Haselton) announced upon information that he had that he was "inclined to recommend that the prayer of the Petitioners be granted."

This petition signed by all thirty-two was then sent to the committee of Lodges, which recommended the dispensation be granted. It was then approved by the Grand Lodge.

Upon receiving the dispensation, the first communication of Tucker Lodge was called to order by Worshipful Master Brother Luther Holt, Senior Warden Brother John Ladd and Junior Warden Brother Harry White on August 24, 1904.

Charter members were Joseph Blake, Sherburne Blake, John Cram, Charles Edgerly, Irwin Folsom, True Gould, Cecil Ham, Luther Holt,

Jonathan Johnson, George Ladd, Harris Ladd, John Ladd, John Prescott, Edwin Poore, Charles Poore, Mark Scribner, Harry White, Carl Whiting, David Whittier and Horace Whittier.

A call came from Most Worshipful Grand Master Ira Arthur Chase ordering Tucker Lodge to assemble its officers for the purpose of being constituted as a regular Lodge on June 26, 1905. The charter was dated May 17, 1905. Tucker Lodge acquired its name from Gilman Henry Tucker, born in Raymond, who later moved to New York City, where he became a prominent publisher of schoolbooks, but according to records, was never a member of Tucker Lodge, nor was any reason stated for naming the Lodge for him.

The meetings were held in the IOOF Hall on Main Street until at a stated communication in April 1919, it was voted by the Lodge to purchase the land and building of D.C. Whittier for $875. This site continues today to be the home of Tucker Lodge.

The Lodge has raised 208 brothers to the sublime degree of master Masons, acquiring many others by transfer and dual membership, and has had thirty-four masters.

Tucker Lodge was honored in 1958–59 by Worshipful Master Robert H. Clement being appointed district deputy grand master of the First Masonic District. As of 1965, the Lodge had 109 members.

The foregoing was authored by Worshipful Brother Clarence Robbins, appointed historian of Tucker Lodge in 1964 by Worshipful Master Josiah Gordon.

Tucker's first traveling assembly to the William Pitt Tavern (the first Masonic Lodge building in New Hampshire, to which Tucker and its members contributed for its restoration, and were therefore charter members) occurred in 1991 for the raising of Brother Robert Forsing to the sublime degree of master Mason, with the assistance of William Whipple (colonial) Military Lodge.

Tucker's first table lodge was served and celebrated during the administration of Worshipful Brother Roland Davis due to the efforts of Brothers Michael Pettengill Sr. and Tad Richardson.

Only Tucker Lodge's second so honored, Right Worshipful John Gordon, served as the First Masonic District deputy grand master in the years 2004 and 2005. He has joined the progression to become the first grand master of Masons for the state of New Hampshire from Tucker Lodge.

The furniture in the Lodge, as well as the three marble markers in South, West and East, were provided by a brother who was also an Odd Fellow. The Odd Fellows Hall was above what is now a convenience store (previous to its being Sanel's Auto Parts, Nickerson's Auto Parts and Holt's Department Store). This can be authenticated by turning the marble blocks over and observing the IOOF inscriptions.

The Lodge master's gavel, the marshalls baton and past masters commemorative wall plaque were designed and produced by long-serving secretary Brother John Aldrich, an outstanding craftsman. The stained-glass "G" in the East was commissioned by Worshipful Master Nelson Sherman and produced by another skilled artist and craftsman, Brother Russell Ege, who also produced the stained-glass square and compass on the exterior wall of the Lodge, commissioned by Worshipful Brother John Stewart.

The year 2011 saw Tucker's first booth at the annual town fair under Worshipful Steven Welch's leadership. In March, lodge members returned to William Pitt to hold a communication. In July, they marched and floated for our first time in the town fair. In December, we had our first breakfast and pictures with Santa.

Masters of Tucker Lodge 1960–2014

Chester E. Menter, 1960–61
George H. Bassett, 1962–63
Josiah R. Gordon, 1963–64
Edward C. Smith, 1965–66
Edward W. Moulton, 1967–68
Donald R. Willoughby, 1969–70
Robert J. Willoughby, 1971–72
John F. Gordon, 1973–74
Wayne A. Ingalls, 1975–76
Ivan C. Reed Jr., 1977–78
Richard A. Nye, 1979–80
George C. Gove, honorary
Nelson E. Sherman, 1981
Chester E. Menter, 1982
Ronald P. Simone, 1983–84
William T. Prince, honorary
John F. Gordon, 1985

John Stewart, 1986–87
Chester E. Menter, 1988
John F. Gordon, 1989
James E. Currier, 1990
Donald R. Willoughby, 1991
Albert G. Henson, 1992–93
Albert J. Henson, 1994
Roland M. Davis, 1995–96
Richard C. Smith, Honorary
Michael V. Pettengill, 1997–98
Warren W. Black, 1999–2000
Roger F. Retzke, 2001–02
Tad W. Richardson, 2003–04
Ryan P. McKinley, 2005–06
Ernest L. Rutherford, honorary
Warren W. Black, 2007
Romeo E. Levesque Jr., honorary
Donald C. Smith Jr., 2008
Craig R. White, 2009
Donald C. Smith Jr., 2010
Steven A. Welch, 2011–12
Oliver P. Frates, 2013
Roger F. Retzke, 2014

The foregoing was authored by Worshipful Brother John Stewart, appointed historian of Tucker Lodge in 1987 by Worshipful Master Roland M. Davis

Veterans of Foreign Wars, Maple-Wheadon Post #4479

By Norman Marcotte

The post was chartered on September 17, 1945. The post building at 39 Main Street was given to the post by Eli N. Marcotte, grandfather of the writer of this article.

The post is required by the national organization to contribute to fifteen charities as well as to local causes.

Commanders of Maple-Weadon VFW Post #4479

Romeo Levesque Sr.,1945–1947
Ernest Cote, 1947–1950
Edgar Smart, 1950
Glen Beachard, 1951
John Roberts, 1952
Herbert Landrigan, 1952–1954
Hardy Hansen, 1955
Anthony Spinazzola, 1956
Emile Quintal, 1957
Edgar Smart, 1958
Herbert Moore, 1959
Dominic Cavalon, 1960
Clarence Robbins, 1961
Charles Piper, 1962
Weston Smith, 1963
Leo Smith, 1964
Oscar St. John, 1965–1967
Clarence Pettengill, 1975–1977
Charles Dember, 1969
Richard Nye, 1970–1972
Fred Horne, 1972–1973
Robert Cotter, 1979
Charles Piper, 1979
Oliver Fugere, 1980–1981
William Landrigan, 1981–1982
James Vassie, 1982–1983
Michael Rooney, 1983–1985
Harry Walton Sr., 1985–1986
Oliver Fugere, 1986–1987
John Martin, 1987–1988
Alan Orff, 1990–1991
Richard Houle, 1991–1992
Phillip Martel, 1992–1993
Walter Palmer, 1993–1999

Norman Marcotte, 1999–2001
Donald Smith, 2001–2009
Norman Marcotte, 2009–2012
Alan Orff, 2012–2013
Frank Reczkowski, 2013–2014

Maple-Wheadon VFW Post #4479 was named in honor of the first men of both World War I and World War II to be killed in action from the Raymond area: Emerson Maple, Chester resident and private of Battery D, 103rd Field Artillery killed near Chateau Thierry, July 20, 1918; and Elmer D. Wheadon, son of Lillie and John Wheadon, a member of the class of 1942 at RHS. His family moved to Raymond in 1938 and owned Cozy Corner market at the corner of Route 156 and Route 101. Sergeant Wheadon was a tail gunner aboard a Flying Fortress that crashed on October 1, 1943, in Switzerland while on a mission to Austria. He was buried in Switzerland on October 4 with other members of his crew. Subsequently, his body was flown to Fall River Depot, Massachusetts, where he was interred in Oak Grove Cemetery in that city. The Purple Heart was awarded to Sergeant Wheadon posthumously.

Raymond Arts

By Susan Hilchey

In 1983, given the momentum of a successful Raymond High School production of *Night Must Fall*, four talented friends established our community theater group, Raymond Arts Associates. Thanks to Ardell Welch, Diana Dawes and Donna Toto of Raymond and David Ramsey of Kingston, Raymond Arts was created.

Raymond Arts followed in the tradition of live performances established by the Hutchinson Summer Theatre. Susan B. Hutchinson planned and designed the one-hundred-seat theater located at the south end of Governor's Lake in Raymond, which opened in 1950 with *Born Yesterday*. The theater featured actors from Boston, New York and local residents in many other performances. After Mrs. Hutchinson's death in 1956, her beloved theater was dark until two New Hampshire natives decided to carry on the tradition. Frank T. Wells and Loren E. Morrill resumed the summer stock from 1962 to 1963, charging two dollars per ticket and obtaining generous support from local businesses. Next, Dr. D.C. Anderson ran the theater from 1967 to 1971; the final show was *Lady Chatterley's Lover*. Later, the playhouse was used as a goat barn until the roof caved in from a heavy snowfall. The remaining theater space has been the private home of Susan Hilchey and Bob Gagnon for over twenty-five years, where Raymond Arts' play readings, rehearsals and meetings have taken place. The Hutchinson family still summers in the former actors' residence next door.

Raymond Arts provides live performances to entertain and bring the community together. The group's first production was *Our Town* on the old high school stage (built in 1938–39 and removed when the new Iber Holmes Gove Middle School was built). Subsequent performances transformed that stage into a court (*Night of January 16*), a Victorian house (*Gaslight*), a summer camp (*On Golden Pond*) and a beauty parlor (*Steel Magnolias*), with wonderful sets to spark the audiences' imaginations. For the 225th town anniversary, Raymond Arts presented *The Children's Hour*.

When the new Raymond High School was built on Harriman Hill Road, performances moved to the high school stage. Many dinner theaters and old favorites were performed over the years, including *Hello Dolly*, *Barefoot in the Park* and *Belles*. Original works by Raymond residents include *Pygmalion, New England Style* by Christy Eppig; *The Magic of Friday Nights* by Jonathan Wood; and *Uncle Frank's Birthday* by Dave Magown. The best publicity for a show occurred for Woody Allen's *Don't Drink the Water*. Upon seeing promotional signs around the town, many residents telephoned the Public Works Department to ask urgently about the problem with the town's drinking water.

Other Raymond Arts activities have included fine art shows, variety shows, town fair skits and a costume photo booth, Arts at Riverside Park, the annual crafts fair and cooperative fund raisers with the VFW/American Legion, Raymond Area Rotary and Raymond schools. Since its inception in 1983, the group has awarded college scholarships to RHS seniors entering the arts profession.

Hutchinson Theatre, a Personal Perspective

By Paul Brown

Susan Hutchinson was a rich lady from Pennsylvania. Her husband, William Seeley Hutchinson, was a part owner of Bethlehem Fabricating Company. They bought a camp on Governor's Pond in the late 1930s. In deference to Bill Hutchinson III, "rich" is by Raymond standards. Bill prefers "well-to-do."

Their daughter, Mary Hutchinson Westland, was an actress in New York City. I never met her but saw a photo of her, and she was very pretty, to my young eyes.

In any case, the family's acting history had something to do with Susan's desire to build a summer theater in Raymond.

In 1950, she built the theater, a large, wood-framed structure attached to her cottage. It was built out over a downhill slope, and the outer end was supported by thick pine posts. That was the stage end. The entrance and ticket office were at the cottage end.

She fashioned a parking area at the lower end of the slope, and graveled and widened Smith Pond Road in some areas. Opening night was July 15, 1950. This date is in my grandmother's diary, as she attended the first night.

And first night was quite successful. She continued plays for several years after that, bringing talent from New York. The plays frequently employed locals in minor parts and as stagehands.

Hutchinson Road is a reminder of Mrs. Hutchinson's determination. A recalcitrant neighbor (my mother) disallowed the removal of a tree that narrowed the road, and Susan purchased land and built the road around the impeding property and tree.

In the late '60s, the property was sold to Delmar Anderson, PhD. Anderson's doctorate was in theater from Boston University. Professor Anderson opted to "drop out" of academia and take on the life of a rusticator in Raymond. His knowledge of theater (perhaps he thought) might bring some culture to the country.

He made a few attempts at bringing plays to the theater, but it didn't seem to pan out for him. Ultimately, he used the theater to house his goats; the building deteriorated and was razed.

The cottage, which had been quite expansive, with several verandas, also deteriorated. He sold the property to Susan Hilchey, who had acted in some of Susan Hutchinson's plays as a child.

13

CULTURAL DIVERSITY

My life spans two eras: the time when agriculture was a major factor in New Hampshire living to the technical age of cellphones and God knows what else of the twenty-first century.

Raymond had about 1,700 souls when I graduated from high school in 1953 and now numbers over 10,000.

Of the 1,700, probably only a few dozen are left, with likely a few hundred children and grandchildren still living in town.

In the 1950s, there were merchants, farmers and factory workers, and not much else. The daily commute to Massachusetts was yet to be.

What was the "culture" in the 1950s? Who were we. And why do I ask this question?

There is a global debate on the subject of "cultural diversity." It seems that the trend is to see minority cultures as endangered and in need of "saving." Others see keeping an Australian Aborigine, for example, in his natural state as depriving him of the comforts and necessities of modern life. Whatever the answer, it should be acknowledged that certain cultural identities are being lost.

A few people would agree with me that there was a time when there was a difference in dialect between Manchester and Raymond.

Several years ago, I went to a memorial service for a longtime Raymond resident, Palmer Hurd. Palmer was a popular guy, and the service was held outdoors at his house. About a half dozen folks offered their remembrances about Palmer, and I was struck with the similarity of the speakers' dialects. They were what I would call "rural New Hampshire."

By "rural," I'm not talking about grammar, but a certain inflection in some words and terms. In fact, educational level doesn't seem to have much to do with the sound.

The *r*'s are missing, as is typical for New England, but there is no compensatory adding of it in the wrong place, as in "Cuber" (Cuba) or "idear" (idea).

The *g*'s are usually deleted, as in "sittin.'" But it's "siT-Tin'" with both *t*'s clearly enunciated, rather than "sitt'n.'"

A friend has an old-fashioned way of saying "Conkid." The same friend also pronounces the word "horses" as "hossiz." The third meal of the day is "suppa."

I'm searching here for a common thread as to a cultural identity in Raymond, then and now. Was it a distinct culture then? What is it now?

I believe that Raymond was a crossroads of sorts. The two shoe factories drew farmers and woodsmen, who were essentially rural, as well as first- or second-generation French from nearby Manchester. Today, you could still find those distinct dialects in certain townspeople.

While those would have been seen as different cultures, with religion (Catholic or Protestant) as the primary difference, attitudes were probably similar. Everyone had to work. There was no free lunch. There was no Catholic school, so all children were educated in the same building and learned from the same books. I think it is safe to say that from the earliest times, there were no noticeable cultural differences.

The merchants were a mix. Greeks ran at least two stores; several were owned by old Raymond names (Blake, Whittier); some by folks from out of state, (Holt, Eccleston); and one was run by Reggie Houle, obviously of French heritage, who married a local woman, Lillian Dockham. The First National and A&P grocery stores were managed by various people, and some were local.

There were folks of African descent, but they were not noticed as such. "African American" was a term yet to be coined, and applying the word "black" to a person would have been considered a pejorative. Racial identity was simply not considered. The "n-word" was not used by polite people. "Colored" was the term used if ever needed.

Now, in the twenty-first century, the "diversity" is undoubtedly greater, but I know of no friction or animosity owed to such.

14

OLD HOUSES

Ages of antique houses tend to be exaggerated. I know of one house that was built in 1832 and was advertised by a realtor as built in 1750. Another in Raymond is shown on the tax assessment as built in 1700, considerably before there were any known settlers in Freetown.

It's possible that the assessment company that did Raymond's revaluation simply designated most of the older homes as "1750," and that designation stands.

There are certain distinguishing characteristics of a particular period in which a home was built. However, those characteristics may be seen on a later house, as an older man may be using the same construction techniques he learned as a teenager.

Experts may be able to estimate the age of a house, but it is only an estimate. Such things as saw marks, boards, beams, construction type and foundations are clues to age.

A relatively new science called dendroarchaeology can tell when a beam was cut, leading to an estimate of age, assuming the beam was not reused from a previous structure.

So in my survey of antique homes in Raymond, I avoid any statements about age because I don't want to contradict a homeowner's opinion, and the most important fact is that nobody really knows the actual age of an antique structure.

Old deeds refer to "the buildings thereon," but it is unknown if they are the same buildings that stand today.

By most accounts, the oldest house in Raymond is the one known as the Bean Tavern, on Old Fremont Road, now owned by Tim and Peg

Louis. According to Fullonton, it is the oldest, and was likely built before incorporation, probably around 1750. It is near the site of the Freetown Mill and an early burying ground. Doubtless, there were other early homes nearby, but they are long gone.

One classic old home that bears mentioning is located on Dudley Road. It was built by Isaac Tucker, probably before 1800. Fullonton describes it at length (see page 131 of his history).

The deed was from Caleb Smith to Tucker in 1786, not mentioning any buildings.

Barbara Beardsley, a talented art conservator and descendant of the Dudley family, formerly resided in one of the Dudley homes on Dudley Road following the death of her mother, Ruth Brooks Hoffman. The land encompasses the site of the Dudley Mill.

The home across the road, owned by David and Kathleen Hoelzel, is a newer version of the original "Dudley Mansion," pictured as a sketch in Fullonton's history.

The Lovering home, on Chester Road, is owned by the heirs of Josiah Gordon. Mr. Gordon was a well-known and respected gentleman and had been a selectman.

And there are two homes on Chester Road, built by the Poors and the Trues. Sally (Guptill) Paradis is descended from both families.

The Jedediah Brown home on Prescott Road is owned by the Rockingham Community Action organization.

There is an early home on Lane Road, owned by the Chandler family. Edgar Chandler was a Congregational pastor in Candia, where his grandfather was once a pastor. He purchased the property in 1940. It appears that an early owner was David Lane, deeded to him in 1763, shown as lot 115, "Old Hundred."

Following is a list of other old homes, by appearance, and I'm sure I'll miss some. And by "older," I mean pre-1850s, with older, post-and-beam construction techniques.

- Cramer residence, Ham Road, once owned by Ham, later by Newton.
- Lovely residence, Ham Road, once owned by Howard, grandparents to Wayne Welch.
- Plante residence, Mountain Road, once owned by Hilliard.
- J&N Revocable Trust, Harriman Hill Road.
- Fullerton residence, Main Street (formerly Arthur and Caroline Severance).
- Landis residence, Main Street (formerly Green).

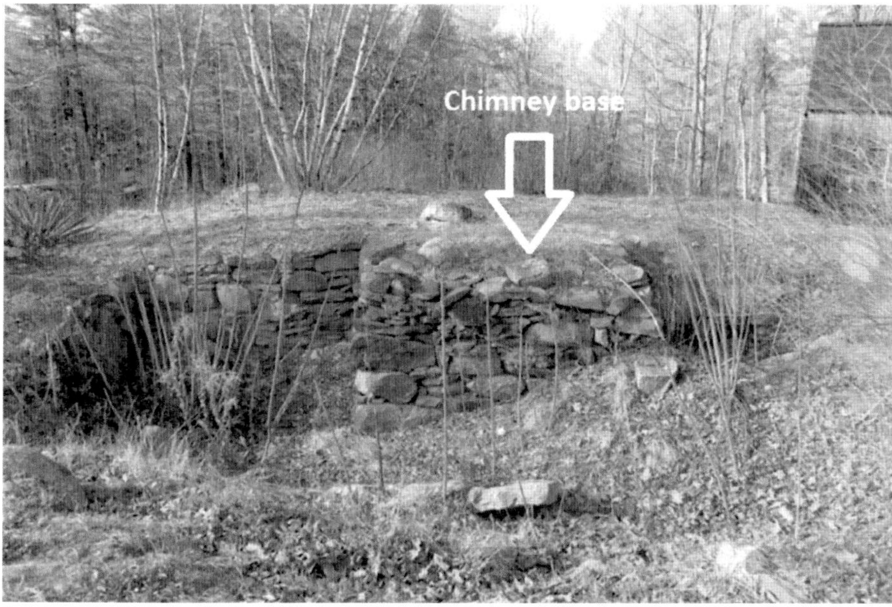

Early foundation. Note small stones used before oxen were available to move larger slabs. *Courtesy of Paul Brown.*

- Winter residence, Epping Street (formerly Whittier).
- Dodge residence, Long Hill Road, originally owned by Tilton.
- Tilley residence, Long Hill Road, once owned by Smith, earlier by Osgood.
- McCoy residence, Long Hill Road, originally owned by Nicolas Gilman.
- Myers residence, Langford Road, once owned by Roscoe Nowell.
- McCosh residence, Onway Lake Road, once owned by Berry.
- Paquin residence, Route 27, near Epping line, was owned by Grace Howard.
- House owned by Bloomfield, Onway Lake Road, near Scribner Road.
- House owned by Nolan, Lane Road.
- House owned by Victoria, Lane Road.
- Capone residence, Batchelder Road, former Batchelder property.
- Degan Residence, Old Fremont Road, once owned by Brown.
- Odom residence, Nottingham Road, former Gove property.
- Winter residence, Nottingham Road, former Cram property.
- O'Connor residence, Nottingham Road, former Folsom property.
- Semple residence, Scribner Road.
- Jason Residence, Blueberry Hill Road.

15

CEMETERIES

When I started writing this chapter, I listed the cemeteries with which I was familiar. Then, after reading the *Pictorial History of Raymond*, in which several other cemeteries were named, I queried Denise O'Grady of our Public Works Department. She kindly provided a map showing a total of twenty-one cemeteries in town. One seems to be missing from the list, named as the "Folsom" cemetery, on Nottingham Road. Due to the publisher's production requirements, the map couldn't be shown here, but it can be seen at the Raymond Public Works office.

There are also a few stones on Brown Road near the intersection with Chester Road. They are in the front yard of a house there.

Town Cemeteries

1. Batchelder (Gile Road)
2. Bean (intersection of Main and Old Fremont Roads)
3. Brown (Prescott Road)
4. Dearborn (Harriman Road, near Philbrick Farm)
5. Dudley Tucker (Dudley Road and Route 27)
6. Green (Dodge-Heath, on Green Road)
7. Ham (Ham Road)
8. Holman (Off Mountain Road)
9. Lane (Lane Road)
10. Launier (Near Ben Moody Farm)
11. Lovering (Chester Road, near Brown Road)
12. Moulton (Main Street, near former Ray Smith garage)

13. Oak Hill (Stage Road?)
14. New Pine Grove (Epping Street)
15. Old Pine Grove (Epping Street)
16. Prescott (Prescott Road)
17. Prevere (Prevere Road)
18. Scribner (Scribner Road, formerly Camp Se-Sa-Ma-Ca)
19. Town line (Actually in Chester)
20. Tucker (Long Hill Road)
21. Winter/Green (Appears to be somewhere off Lane Road near Green)

Some of these cemeteries are on private property. The property owners should be approached for permission to visit any cemetery. For example, a deed allows heirs of the Tucker family to cross, by the driveway, the present owners' property to enter the Tucker cemetery on Long Hill.

Cemeteries from 1857 County Map

Note that the cemetery is located near the Common, and the Methodist Church is where the Catholic Church would be at a later time. The cemetery was moved to make room for the library.

The following is quoted from page 281 of Fullonton's work:

> *Ichabod's second son, Henry, lived in Hampton Falls, and married Abigail Butler, Oct. 9, 1734. Their oldest son was Daniel, born Jan 9, 1735, who came to Raymond after 1760, and settled on the spot where the writer resides. He died, April 27, 1795 and was buried in the field a little way south of George S. Robie's on the west side of the road. On a common flat stone, at the head of the grave, is the following inscription. We preserve the spelling, the only specimen of the sort we have seen in town. There are many in New England, which is not strange, as in early times education was limited.*
>
> *HEAR LIES THE*
> *BODY OF DANIEL*
> *ROBIE DYED IN THE*
> *YERS 1795 AG 57 YRS*
> *AP 27*

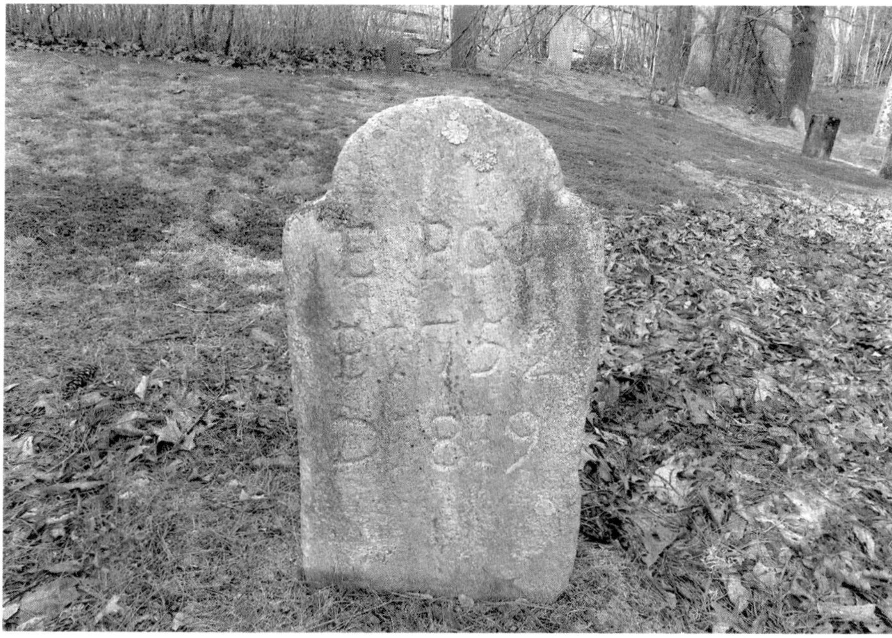

An early, primitive gravestone in Bean Cemetery. *Courtesy of Paul Brown.*

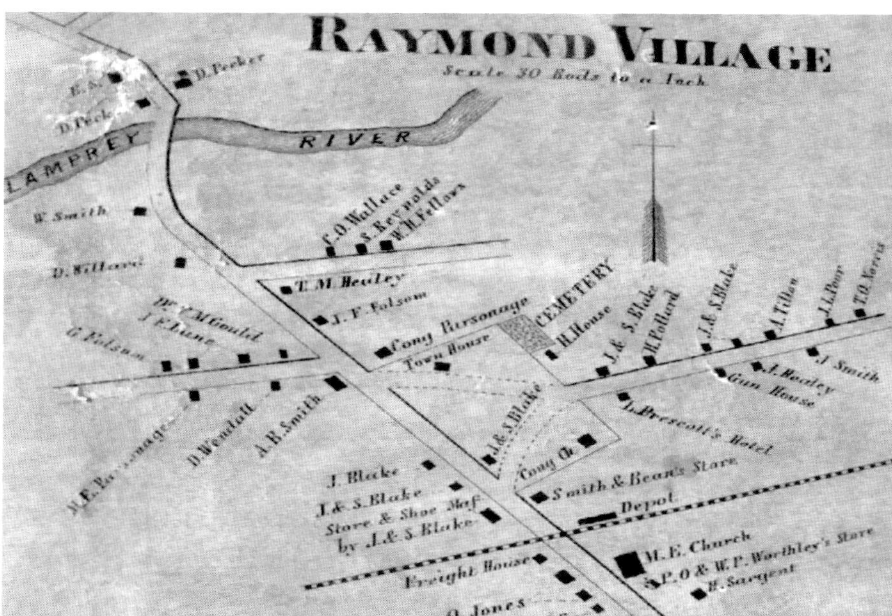

Detail of an 1856 map showing village and cemetery in location of future library.

Since reading this tidbit when I was a teenager, I wondered about the whereabouts of that stone. I had guessed that its location was on Freetown Road somewhat south of the Raymond Shopping Center. I queried Ramona Stevens, a president of the Raymond Historical Society; she, in turn, queried Loren Welch, who lived nearby. The second-hand answer was vague.

More recently, I discussed a number of details with Barry Dunphy, who was Loren Welch's nephew. Barry commented that he had seen a stone with a date on it as Route 101 was being completed. So it is highly likely that Mr. Robie's remains are beneath Route 101 approximately on the westerly side of the overpass at Freetown Road.

Finally, Fullonton mentions Joseph Dudley, who operated a mill and lived near the Griffin mill site, which is across the road from the Pines restaurant. Fullonton says that Mr. Dudley died in 1792 and was buried a little to the east, "with others" in "the pasture now owed by Oliver Tilton."

Oliver Tilton lived where Sumner and Shirley Dodge reside. That farm originally extended down to the river, which leaves another unmarked burial ground somewhere near the building housing the Raymond Animal Hospital. That is, near or under it, or the highway, or another building, or...

16

HISTORY OF RANGES AND LOTS

BY PAUL BROWN

Property boundaries are evidence of Raymond's early days and the original proprietors.

As most people know, Raymond was once part of Chester. Chester was granted to people from Hampton, Portsmouth and Exeter who envisioned settlements in a "waist land" to the west of Exeter and north of Kings Towne.

They appointed surveyors to plot out lots for settlers in what is now Chester, and later, in 1728, decided to plot out the "North Parish," or "Freetown," into lots to be divvied up among the grantees.

The lots were to be one hundred acres in size, later known as "Old Hundred Acre Lots," or "Old Hundred."

A mill was already in operation on the Lamprey, probably somewhat upstream of the bridge on Freetown Road. There was a road to the mill from Exeter, which bordered Raymond, because Epping was not yet a separate town.

Apparently, there was no surveyor's licensing board at the time, because the drawing of the lots on paper didn't always match the facts on the ground. There were several maps made, but the one that has survived and is used to this day by surveyors was drawn by Benjamin Chase for his *History of Old Chester*. That map and Chase's history are available online.*

---

*The New Hampshire Historical Society has a range and lot map of Raymond, dated 1771, which is probably more accurate than Chase's.

For the edification of some of my readers who might be interested, I am including a portion of Chase's map, showing the "Old Hundreds" and a list of the grantees for the lots.

The reader will note, when reading Chase, that the lots are divided into divisions and ranges. There are "rangeways" between groups of lots, also called "reserves," for roads. Some of our present roads, but very few, are along the rangeways. And frequently, when two parallel stone walls are seen a few feet apart, they may be marking an ancient rangeway.

About half of the lots in Raymond have a northeast–southwest orientation. When examining the tax map, one can easily see the original range and lot lines.

As an example, note the parallel stone walls between 4 and 6 Main Street, near Route 27. Those walls appear on the other side of Route 27, between 135 and 137 Route 27, and the line forms the rear bound of the properties on the northwest side of Sesame Street.

Picture a surveyor pacing off fifty rods for the front of a lot, hacking a mark on a tree and then pacing off to the next one. These lots were granted to the original proprietors, who then sold their lot to someone else, simply describing "my lot in the waist land." Later, visualize the purchaser, an early settler wandering around the woods and swamps, looking for the tree with the mark. Undoubtedly, the confusion resulted in more than a few disputes about title. I assume there might have been some yelling, which may be where the term "quiet title" came from.

Interestingly, I note that the area now encompassing the Raymond Transfer Station, formerly known as "the town dump," was first granted to the colonial governor, Benning Wentworth.

The list of original proprietors is contained in the table on the following pages:

Name	Lot
Philemon Blake	124
James Boyd	85
Abraham Brown	129
George Brownell	46
Nathaniel Bachelder Sr.	122
Jonathan Brown	47
Moses Blake	77

Name	Lot
Samuel Blake	139
Josiah Batchelder	137
Nathaniel Batchelder Jr	23
Joseph Batchelder	69
Jacob Basford	107
John Calfe	43
Amos Cass	10
Richard Clifford	20
Zachariah Clifford	15
Jonathan Clough	128
Reverend Theophilus Cotton	50
John Cram	113
William Crosswait	116
Cutts and Akerman	108
William Daniels	75
Thomas Dean	106
Jonathan Dearborn	136
Ebenezer Dearborn	64
Ephraim Dennet	86
Abraham Drake	53
Nathaniel Drake	78
Ebenezer Eastman	62
Edward Emerson	24
Jonathan Emerson	81
James Failes	131
*Reverend Ebenezer Flagg	
James Fogg	4
Benoni Fogg	8

Name	Lot
Robert Ford	44
Benjamin Gambling, Esq..	9
Jacob Garland	83
Jacob Gilman	3
Major John Gilman	28
Edward Gilman	35
William Godfrey	30
Ephraim Guile	33
Richard Haseltine	19
William Healey	110
Reverend Moses Hale	80
Clement Hughes	29
Colonel Mark Hunking	102
Samuel Ingalls	74
George Jaffrey, Esq.	40
John Jaquish	36
Richard Jaquish	135
Stephen Johnson	100
Captain Richard Kent	6
Jonathan Kimball	63
Thomas Leavitt	16
John Littlehale	123
Ebenezer Loverell	17
Samuel Marston	2
Captain Archibald McPhedris	99
Clement Messervy	73
Luther Morgan	114
Colonel Thomas Packer	140

Name	Lot
Samuel Page	52
John Packer	91
Parsonage lots	90
Samuel Penhallow, Esq.	57
James Perkins	133
Thomas Phipps, Esq.	95
Captain Joshua Pierce	21
Captain Thomas Pierce	5
George Pierce	39
Jonathan Plummer	79
John Prescutt	25
John Prescutt Jr.	126
James Prescutt	130
Samuel Prescutt	96
Ichabod Roby	82
Reverend Nathaniel Rogers	111
Robert Row	45
Eleazer Russell	38
Captain William Rymes	58
Joseph Sanborn	92
Nathaniel Sanborn	31
Benjamin Sanborn	117
Reuben Sanborn	54
John Sanborn	127
Enoch Sanborn	27
Edward Sanborn	120
Captain Jonathan Sanborn	48
Jerry Sanborn	59

Name	Lot
School lots	89
John Shackford	55
Samuel Shackford	119
Captain Henry Sherburne	49
Samuel Sherburne	109
Captain Joseph Sherburne	56
Deacon Samuel Shaw	37
John Silly	1
Reverend Thomas Simms	105
Thomas Silver	22
Susannah Small	76
Thomas Smith	18
Benjamin Smith	132
Elisha Smith	51
Samuel Smith	103
Captain Henry Sloper	97
Jacob Stanian	66
Stephen Sweat	26
Captain Joseph Tilton	7
David Tilton	134
Jethro Tilton	72
Samuel Thompson	65
Philip Towie	42
Benjamin Towle	60
Caleb Towle	12
Colonel Shadrack Walton	112
Colonel Peter Weare	11
Nathan Webster	13
Stephen Webster	61

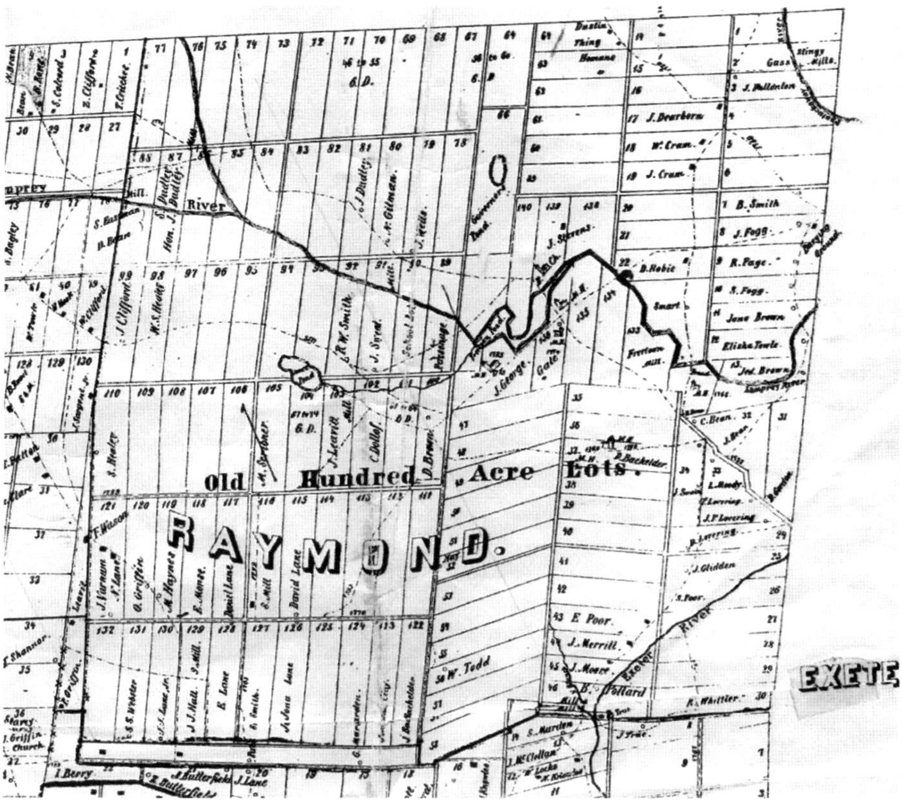

See next page for captions

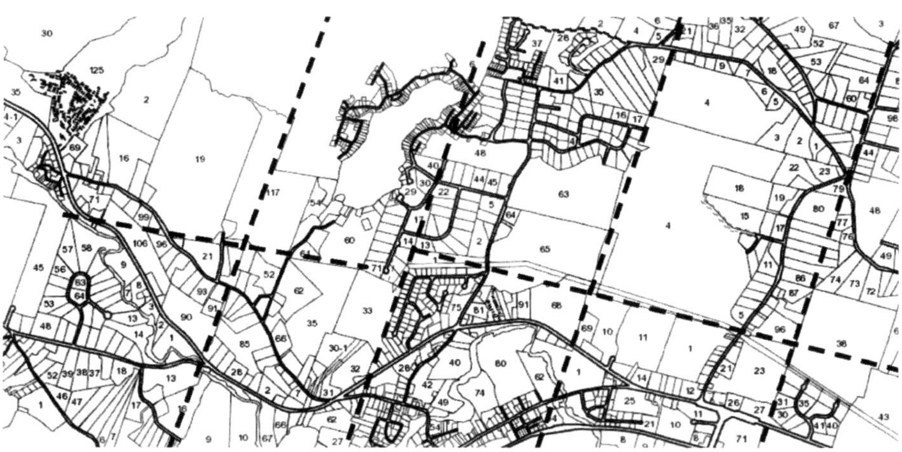

Name	Lot
Capt. Ebenezer Wentworth	68
Benning Wentworth	32
Michael Whidden	41
Thomas Whiting	34
William White	138
Captain Richard Wibird	14
Captain Joshua Wingate	84
Colonel Thomas Westbrook	115
Henry Works	118
Joseph Young	121

Page 155, top: This map is from Benjamin Chase's *History of Old Chester*. Chase has drawn in early roads in Raymond. An early road from 1758 was from Freetown Mill to Dudley Mill. It followed Main Street from Freetown Road, Long Hill Road to Route 27 and a bit of Deerfield Road to Dudley Road. The beginning was an old road lying between the probable site of Freetown Mill and Main Street. It can be seen on topographical maps and the tax map.

The intersection of Freetown and Nottingham Roads are offset now at Route 27. Originally, it may have been straight across Route 27, as prior to the development of Walgreen and Irving, there were two parallel stone walls between the two properties.*

Page 155, bottom: Part of Raymond's tax map. The lines I have drawn on this map show the three rangeways and groups of lots in the northeast corner of town. There is an inconsistency in Chase's map and his table of grantees. The map shows the school lot and the parsonage lot to be reversed. Deeds show the table to be correct.

*Hazel Littlefield wrote that this was the road to Concord.

17

BAD STUFF

Homicides

I suppose every little New Hampshire town has experienced some violence. Raymond is no exception, but there have been very few homicides over the years.

The earliest I can think of in my lifetime was the untimely death of Ernest Dudley, whose body was found outside the restaurant owned at the time by a Tobias, later called the Long Branch. There might have been a brawl, but no one seemed to know what had happened to the young man. To my knowledge, no one was ever prosecuted for this incident. This happened in the 1940s. Dudley was married to a young woman by the name of Marjorie (Cammett) and left three young children.

The following is an excerpt from a ruling by the New Hampshire Supreme Court dated December 6, 1995. I have added the defendant's name.

> *On June 27, 1992, Joanna Kozak left her residence in Fremont to go for a dirt bike ride with the defendant* [Steven Roy]. *She never returned. At the time of her death, Kozak shared the residence with, among others, the defendant and Maria Zarate, the mother of two of the defendant's children. When Kozak failed to return from the dirt bike ride, the defendant told Zarate that Kozak, then a fugitive from justice, had packed her belongings and left the residence permanently.*

Weeks later, the defendant confided to Zarate that on June 27, 1992, he had bludgeoned Kozak to death. He also stated that he had buried her body in an isolated cemetery and disposed of her belongings with the assistance of C.J. Kelley.

On October 10, 1992, Zarate decided to permanently leave the Fremont residence. While waiting at the Manchester Airport, she made an anonymous telephone call to the Epping Police Department informing them that "a crime had been committed" at the Scribner Cemetery in Raymond. In November 1992, Zarate was interviewed by the FBI. As a result, Kozak's body was discovered on December 10, 1992, by the New Hampshire State Police.

On March 16, 1993, C.J. Kelley gave a tape recorded statement to the New Hampshire State Police. C.J. Kelley stated that the defendant had killed Kozak, and admitted that he helped the defendant bury the body. He was subsequently indicted for his role in assisting the defendant to conceal Kozak's murder. On April 12, 1993, the defendant was arrested and charged with first degree murder. Zarate was the State's lead witness.

Murder Solved?

On May 5, 1974, Walter "Scud" Lyman was found dead in his two-room cottage on Old Manchester Road. He had been savagely beaten and stabbed three times. The news shocked the town, and the hunt was on to find the murderer.

Scud was a small, wiry man, and he had been elected Raymond's chief of police from 1936 to 1941. One of my early memories was of my bad behavior prompting threats to send Scud Lyman after me.

He was a colorful character. I heard stories that he made moonshine during Prohibition. He was known as an excellent baseball player, playing for a semipro farm team.

In his older years, he did odd jobs for the town, in particular mowing the grass in the Common and keeping it tidy.

The crime was investigated by the Raymond Police Department, the Rockingham Sheriff's Department and the state police. A command center was set up in the upper level of the fire station.

A reward was established by his son-in-law; the first gift was $1,000, not a paltry sum in those days.

Rumors abounded that there was a suspect. One of the places to follow up rumors was Gordon Cammett's store on Main Street. Gordon was a selectman, his wife, Helen, was a sister to the chief of police, J. Henry Greenwood.

I asked Helen if there was any new news about Scud's untimely demise.

Her answer was another question: "What's *your* name?"

It became apparent that the suspect's name was very similar to mine.

Was the murder ever solved?

The answer is "Probably."

In my research for this book, I asked Chief David Salois about the case. He referred me to Sergeant Scott Payne, who had the "cold case file" and was still investigating the crime that had taken place thirty-seven years earlier and before he, Sergeant Payne, was born.

Sergeant Payne divulged that there had been a confession soon after the murder. The suspect's confession described the crime scene and details that only the killer would know. Then the suspect recanted.

Scud Lyman probably knew his killer. The man had previously stayed in Scud's home while Scud visited his daughter in the south. At the time of the murder, the suspect was on the run from the youth detention center and sought refuge in Scud's home. Scud objected, perhaps by attacking the intruder. The suspect, enraged, put an end to Scud's life. It was said at the time that "Scud put up one hell of a fight."

One might ask if justice has ever been meted out to the alleged killer. Recently, he has met his maker, and it is not for this material world to decide.

The Raymond Common is formally known as the "Walter Lyman Park."

The following is an excerpt from an article by James A. Kimble in the *New Hampshire Union Leader* recounting some detail about the murder of Robert Scott Dickinson in 2012:

> *BRENTWOOD—A Raymond man charged with killing 50-year-old Robert "Scott" Dickinson sold his victim's bass guitar and even offered up his jacket for sale at a pawn shop hours after the murder, according to New Hampshire State Police.*
>
> *Damien Tisbert, who was indicted last month on a first-degree murder charge, also told a friend in Manchester on the night of March 25 that "he was having problems with his schizophrenia" and that "he was going to jail for the rest of his life," court records say.*
>
> *A review of recently unsealed search warrants and affidavits indicate that police found several witnesses who interacted with Tisbert just after he allegedly killed Dickinson and bragged about it to friends.*

Dickinson was found severely beaten and stabbed numerous times with his throat slit inside his home at 14 Floral Ave. in Raymond.

The murder happened in the early morning hours of March 25 after Dickinson had an exchange with his estranged wife, Malissa, who was dating Tisbert's father, according to state police.

Dickinson's mother, Carol, found her son's body and promptly called 911.

State police received a break in the case when Tisbert's friends and co-workers began coming forward the day after Dickinson's homicide, saying that Tisbert claimed that he murdered someone, according to the documents.

Those witnesses include Jessica Dunn, a high school acquaintance who Tisbert had taken inside Dickinson's home right after the murder to sleep in an upstairs bedroom, state police said.

She and Michael Yanz told investigators that they traveled with Tisbert to a pawn shop in Litchfield earlier in the day, state police said.

Tisbert received $20 for the bass guitar but the store refused to buy a Harley-Davidson jacket that authorities believe belonged to Dickinson, state police Sergeant John Encarnacao said in an affidavit.

Tisbert apparently stayed up all night after killing, and went to a bonfire near his father's home on Epping Street between 4:00 and 5:00 a.m. after parting ways with Dunn, state police said.

Scott Haskell, who was at the fire, told police that Tisbert came by and asked for a cigarette lighter. Haskell noticed blood on Tisbert's sneakers, and when he pointed it out, Tisbert responded "that he was up drinking all night and didn't remember what had happened," a police affidavit says.

"Tisbert also pulled out a pair of brass knuckles which had blood on them," state trooper William Bright said in a sworn affidavit.

Mr. Tisbert has pleaded guilty as of this writing and will be serving a prison term.

18
ODD STUFF

Big Rocks, Big Trees

Many folks will remember the two huge boulders astride Route 107, Deerfield Road, just north of Dudley Road. The road was winding and quite scenic. The state, however, felt that making the road safer was a priority, so the boulders were blasted apart and the road straightened and widened.

A citizens' petition was presented to the state when the "improvement" was announced, but the highway department averred that it was never received.

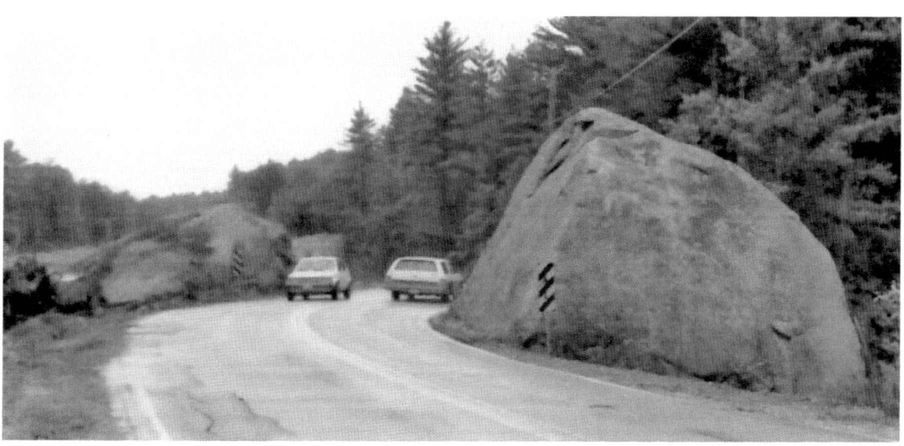

These boulders sat astride Deerfield Road just north of Dudley Road. *Courtesy of Paul Brown.*

The Great White Rock

By Sally Paradis

Mention of Raymond's great White Rock somehow escaped the interest of earlier authors of Raymond history, but not of residents of earlier generations and particularly to youngsters who grew up in the lower Main, Moulton Street or Orchard Street areas. They traversed the wooded area frequently, seeking out the glacial boulder. Once there, they stood in awe, looking up at the colossal remnant of the ice age that swept through this part of New Hampshire centuries ago.

Though we were forbidden by our parents "never to go to White Rock without an adult along," it was, nevertheless, exciting to gather a few friends on the first warm day in spring and disappear from the neighborhood up Standpipe Hill at the end of Orchard Street. There the trek would begin through the woods to see if this giant wonder of the world was still present.

White Rock was but a forgotten childhood memory when this writer happened to find a book in a Naples, Florida bookstore in 2006. The title, *New Hampshire—Off the Beaten Path*, aroused my curiosity as to what it might have to say about our fair Raymond. I scanned the table of contents, and there, on page 23 in the seacoast section, was an article titled "Missing: A 48-Foot White Rock." Spot on. It was about our treasure in Raymond!

The authors had described it as follows: "It is 48 feet long, 39 feet wide, and from 24–30 feet high. Two pine trees have become lodged in crevices." According to the authors, Barbara Radcliffe Rogers and Stillman Rogers, they visited Raymond to look for the White Rock, but all the people they asked "were stumped." They encouraged readers to give them directions or tell them when and how it disappeared so that these could be included in their next edition.

My first reaction was one of complete disbelief. How could the authors write about this landmark without locating it? Similarly, how could not a single person in town who was queried know about the existence of the White Rock? (Perhaps someone knew but did not wish to reveal its location.) Alas, the authors left town, thinkig perhaps that the White Rock had "disappeared."

Soon thereafter, with a friend and camera in hand, we took the steep uphill climb through heavy underbrush buttressed with very tall trees to the spot. Yes, the great White Rock was still there, just as awesome as ever! Perhaps the white surface had become tarnished over the years from its surroundings or from that which had fallen out of the sky over the years.

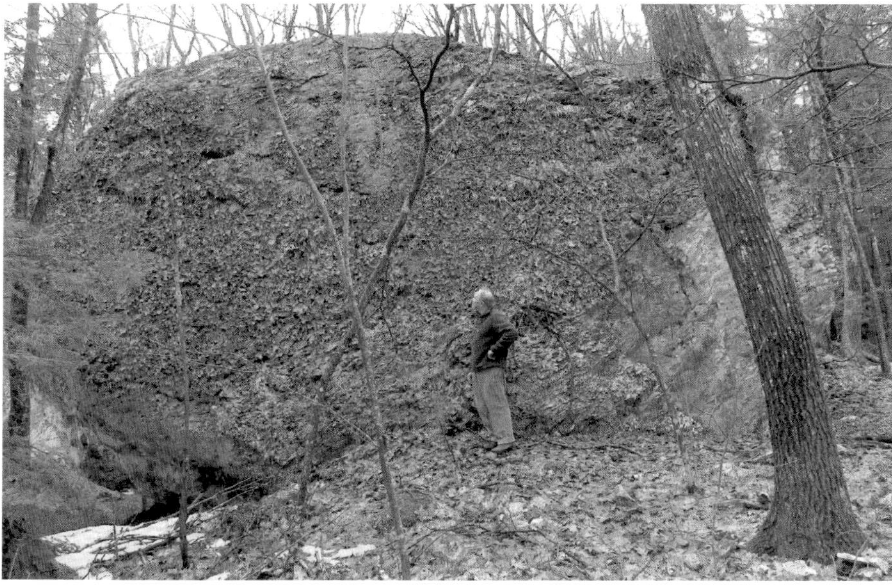

The "Great White Rock." *Courtesy of Paul Brown.*

Still evident and in place was the large ledge-like aperture midway up the southerly side of the rock. This lean-to arrangement had provided shelter for a flock of Moulton family sheep that did not make it home from pasture due to the early onset of an extremely harsh winter nearly a century ago. When the spring thaw allowed access to search for the flock, family members were relieved—a few sheep had perished, but the majority had survived the winter, sheltered by the great White Rock.

Big Trees

There are probably many denizens of the deep forests that rooted during the forest's habitation by the Indians, but two that bear mention and that are easy to see are located at the rear of Raymond High School and near 10 Long Hill Road.

A seventy-four-foot-high chestnut oak is located behind the high school. Listed as a Champion in the New Hampshire Register of Big Trees, it remains the state's largest recorded living specimen of its species as of November 1, 1989. There is also a huge oak located on Long Hill Road.

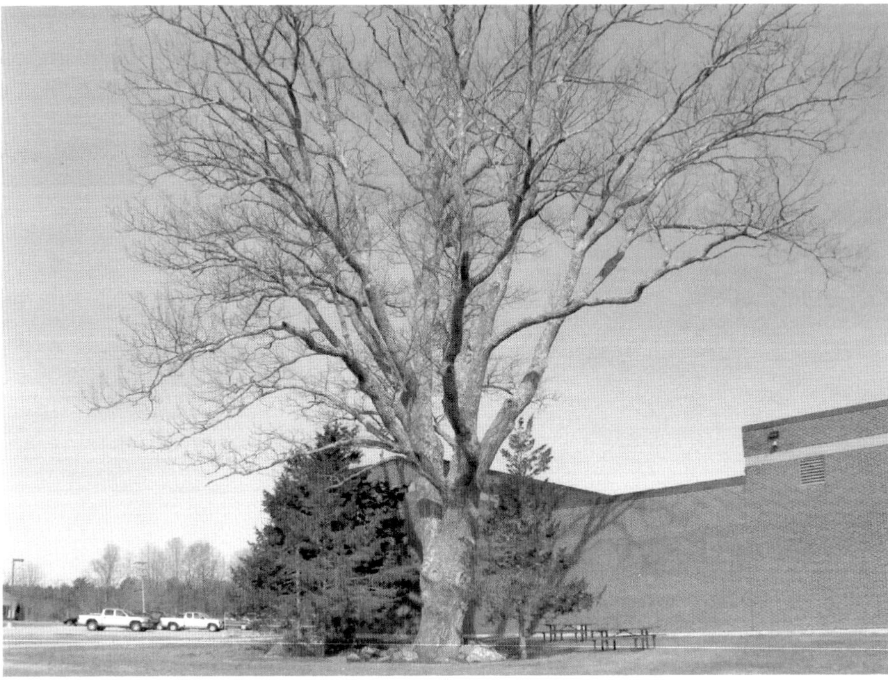

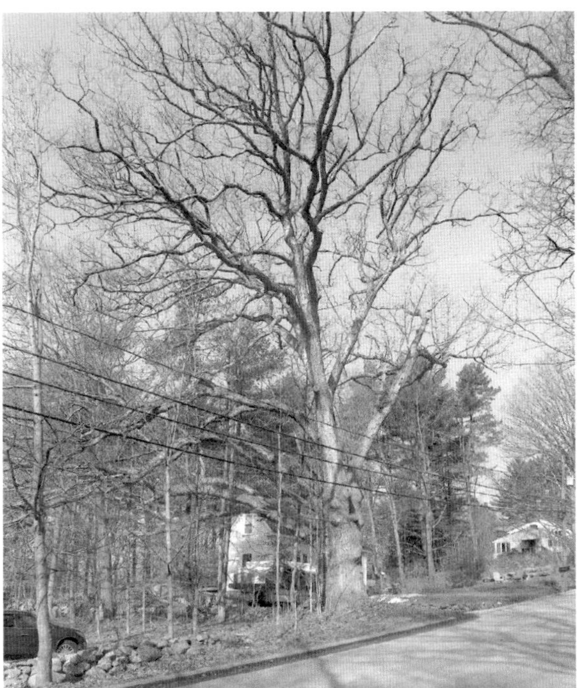

Above: Big chestnut oak behind Raymond High School. *Courtesy of Paul Brown.*

Left: Big oak on Long Hill Road. *Courtesy of Paul Brown.*

The Slogan Contest

I think it fortunate that Raymond never makes it into national or international news, given the news's belief that "if it bleeds, it leads"—that is, there's not too much bloodshed in Raymond.

In the summer of 2009, a subcommittee of the Raymond Business and Economic Development Council hit on a plan to develop some positive publicity for the town, with the hopes of drawing business.

The plan, simply enough, was a "Worldwide Slogan for Raymond" contest. Anyone in the world could offer a slogan and plagiarism was OK; there were no rules.

Diane Janusz, one of the two subcommittee members (I was the other) had an inspiration. Drawing on Raymond's agricultural past and looking forward to its technological future, her first slogan offering was "Raymond: Where the Manure Hits the Wind Turbine."

This was presented to the board of selectman at a Monday night meeting.

The next day, the New Hampshire Union Leader carried the banner headline, including a little sign proclaiming: "Raymond: Where the Manure Hits the Wind Turbine."

The news item brought mixed opinions. Most thought it was funny. Some objected to the obvious reference to an old saying. But the contest was on.

Mrs. Janusz was contacted by WMUR-TV for an interview that was cancelled because of an invasion somewhere.

Shortly afterward, I was called by PBS for an interview on *All Things Considered*, which gave us a national venue. A week or so later, I had a telephone interview with New Zealand's version of PBS.

The result was hundreds of slogan offerings by e-mail from throughout the United States and New Zealand.

The contest winner, we promised, would receive a standing ovation from the board of selectmen and an autographed picture of Senator Jack Barnes. We hinted that the winner might be on *Oprah*, although we acknowledged that Oprah didn't know about it, yet.

There were four judges: Mrs. Janusz, Superintendent Jeanne Richards, a high school senior and myself. We each listed our four choices on a sheet of paper taped to the wall.

One slogan was common to all four lists: "Friendly Faces, Scenic Places—Raymond." The winner was Evelyn Schroeder from Candia, right next door. Ms. Schroeder received the ovation from the select board, her autographed photo of our good Senator Barnes and a lot of congratulations.

I was told that, unfortunately, a member of the board of selectmen "didn't like" the slogan, and it has never been incorporated.

Some Funny Things Happened on the Way Here

(Thanks to Matthew "Sandy" Thomas, who reminded me of these tidbits)

In the early 1970s, there was an overture from Aristotle Onassis, a Greek shipping magnate, to build an oil refinery in the Durham area. The plan was to offload oil at the Isles of Shoals and pipe it through Great Bay. Organized opposition brought the idea to a halt. Onassis, incidentally, had married Jacqueline Kennedy, the widow of the president, but didn't get to have his way with Rockingham County.

In the mid-1970s, a Theodore Caras proposed a refinery for Raymond, using the B&M rail line for the pipeline route. This plan also met with stiff resistance and was abandoned.

In April 1995, a promoter by the name of Mark O. Hildonen proposed a sports and entertainment complex in the area of Exit 4. It seemed to be really simple: buy 267 acres of land in thirteen parcels from eight property owners. Known as "the Quadroplex," it would have a professional hockey team and, Hildonen predicted, would be the location of the 2014 Winter Olympics. A special town meeting was held in the high school gym. At the meeting, Mr. Hildonen, then known as "Marco," pitched his plan.

Most folks thought it a good idea, including this writer. After all, $110 million means a lot of jobs and could make a sizeable dent in property tax bills.

Hindsight, however, suggests that Marco didn't have the money, nor did he even know where he could get it. Word got back to Raymond alleging that he had attempted to scam a North Carolina man out of a $25 million rare ruby.

So far as we know, "Marco" never came back to Raymond. He still owes the town $5,000 for the special meeting.

In the spring of 2004, Sam, a golden retriever, escaped from his home in Candia. He was seen in several area towns, but avoided attempts to capture him. Sam stayed on the run for two years, had one collision with a car, dodged deer hunters and dealt with ticks and various other woodsy perils. Officer Tona McCarthy of the Raymond Police Department resolved to end Sam's sojourn.

With assistance from NHSPCA investigator Steve Sproul, Officer McCarthy rigged a trap that finally ended the "Golden Ghost's" years on the run. Officer McCarthy says that Sam was happily wagging his tail as soon as he was in custody. The cookies that the good officer carries in his pocket might have helped.

19
RETROSPECTIVES OF RAYMOND

Down Memory Lane

By Hazel Littlefield (March 1999)

I was born April 24, 1909, in a house where the road to Fremont and Chester crossed. I lived on the Batchelder Road until I was four and then moved to the house on Epping Road (the Cram house, now the premises of the miniature golf course). The grass grew up in the middle of Epping Road, later Route 101, now Route 27. The house just east of this one was a stagecoach inn (now Irving Gas), and between the two houses was a dirt road that went to Concord.

There were two stores by the Blake brothers, one a grocery and the other a grain store, run by Hattie Woodman and Triff Brusso. There was an "all things" store run by Edgar Brown, and in the back of the store was an undertaking room. Jimmy, the Blind Man's store, was located across the railroad tracks. Also Albert Elliot's, attached to his house at the corner of Epping and School Streets, with a pigpen below it. There was also a five-cent ice cream cone at the Fruit Store owned by the Fasekis family and a bakery on Main Street that sold cakes, donuts and lollipops for one cent.

The railroad station was very important and brought our mail and took us to Manchester. A good old steam engine came through to Manchester in the morning and back at night.

The schools were in districts—Gile, Gove, Pecker and Scribner. I attended the Pecker school located on Main Street across from Harriman Road—two rooms with an outhouse in the back. I moved to the Consolidated School, and there were thirteen in my graduating class.

There were several garages in town (Willoughby's and Maynard's come to mind) as people replaced the horse and buggy with an automobile. The first car I ever saw was Dr. Guptill's. He had a driver and visited patients in their homes. His office was on Main Street, and we paid one dollar for an office call. Dr. Guptill brought a lot of us into the world. I remember whenever he came to the house, he would take out his comb and fix his beautiful head of hair. He predicted that the center of town would be where the Raymond Shopping Center is located, and it has come to pass! Dr. Pollard, the dentist, had an office in his home on Epping Street.

Memorial Day (we called it Decoration Day) was wonderful. We schoolchildren always dressed in our best and marched down to the cemetery. A veteran would take us around to veterans' graves, and we would put a flag on them. Then we marched back to the Common, had dinner at the Odd Fellows Hall and then went back to the Common, where there were speakers and a band concert. It was a nice day. The Raymond Band played on the Common every month during warm weather.

We had movies every Friday night upstairs in the Odd Fellows Hall. We all looked forward to that and to the serial that continued from week to week. The movies were run by the Thayer brothers from Epping, Jerry and Oliver. The movies were silent, and Mary Briggs played a piano located at the foot of the stage. Oliver also played the drums and Jerry, a violin. It cost us twenty-five cents. Then later, the movies had sound.

I found the library (at its present location) when I was about six years old, and from then on, I was a steady patron. I loved to read and still do. There were two churches, the Congregational and the Methodist. We were a Methodist family and continue to be. We made red flannel hash following our harvest dinner each fall, and the shoe workers would buy it to bring home for their supper. The first Methodist minister I recall was a Mr. Young, who also taught school to make a living.

There was an open field where Hampton Machine Co. is now located. Every summer, the gypsies would camp there. I was afraid because people said they would steal children. The New Hampshire National Guard camped there in the summer, too. I was glad to see them. That tract of land was a trotting park for Dr. Guptill's horses and ponies. These were truly the good old days!

The firemen had a ball every winter and the whole town turned out. This was at the Odd Fellows Hall. I can see Mr. Holmes and his wife leading the grand march. Once in a while, there was a talent show in the hall. The "old firehouse" was the one I remember as always being where it is now. The firemen worked in the shoe shops, and they would leave every time the shop whistle blew.

The Grange, Masons, Odd Fellows and Rebekahs were the organizations in town.

Most people did their banking in Manchester. Now we have three banks in Raymond.

Raymond had a baseball team. It played in a field between Orchard Street and the railroad tracks. I remember one player, Walter "Scud" Lyman. I was pretty small and went with my sister. In later years, Scud was the police chief, but the first chief I remember was Edwin Dudley.

Lake Onway was a very popular vacation spot. The train stopped in the summer, and people came from all around to stay at the Batchelder House. On the other side of the lake were the Moody and Berry guesthouses. There was also Smith Pond, now known as Governor's Lake, and Loon Pond near the Epping line. A part of the Lamprey River near Frank Corson's place (new location of the CAP center) was called "Dead Pond."

Behind the barn in the field where I grew up on Epping Street, there was an apple orchard with many kinds of that fruit, including Russets, King Tompkins, Porters, Pumpkin Sweets, Baldwins and crabapples.

We had a "pack" peddler that came on the train from Manchester, carrying a suitcase in each hand and one on his back, selling thread, cloth and other necessities. A ragman came and gathered your grain bags filled with rags, and a broom man came with a variety of brooms for sale. The Raleigh man came with his horse and wagon carrying ointments, shoe polish, flavorings and much more. He stayed at our house while covering Raymond with his wares.

In winter, the roads were plowed by a horse with a wooden plow. There were many big drifts.

Town meeting was held in the Odd Fellows Hall, all on the same day. There was a lot of arguing going on but the next day everything was forgotten.

All the houses had an outhouse. Most were separate from the main building. Oil lamps supplied our lighting—there was no electricity. Most people burned wood in their stoves before coal became available. Electric lights came into being, as did bathrooms. Then the telephone came, and we could speak to nearly everyone. I worked as an operator for several years. The telephone office was run by Clara Brown and her daughter Georgia. There were so few numbers I remembered them all.

Eli Marcotte ran a barge (truck) with bench seats along the side to Hampton Beach in the summer. I went there a few times. It was a great treat.

During World War I, a lot of the young Raymond men went into the service. During that time, the flu epidemic hit many local people, and many of them died.

In between the fruit store and bank was Charlie Bates's livery stable. He rented out horses and wagons, and you could also put up your horse there while you worked in the shoe shop. There were two shoe shops, the big one and the little one.

On the other side of the fruit store, still on Main Street, Mrs. Staples ran a restaurant. Food was also served at the Pilgrim Inn, both patronized mostly by local people and by a few salesmen coming into town by train.

There was an icehouse along the river's edge, and each winter, ice was cut and stored in the icehouse. Everyone had an icebox to use in the summer.

The Pecker Bridge flooded over every spring. Someone had a boat, and he would carry people across morning and night so that they could get to work at the shoe shop.

The Smart's bridge, as it was called, on Epping Road used to overflow in front of the "new cemetery." I walked up the railroad tracks, over the covered bridge, to go to work at the telephone office.

There was and still is a watering trough at the common near the Methodist Church. I have fond memories of "old Prince" drinking there. I hope that it will always be left there.

The Good Old Days

By Charlena (Littlefield) Thompson

I arrived at my home on Orchard Street off Main Street in 1926. It was near the hill where the first tall water tank was built. That water tank and the steeple of the Methodist Church are the two tallest structures in town.

Off Orchard Street, a left turn went into Moulton Street, which continued back to Main Street. Within that area lived many friends with whom I played and walked to school.

The middle school, with all its changes and additions, is in the spot where we attended school for twelve years. There was no kindergarten then. The school day was from nine to four with an hour off at noon. The students who lived far away and had to be bussed brought lunches. Later, we had a cafeteria, and hot lunches were served. Because I lived within walking distance, I went home for lunch.

In 1939, we were happy to see the gymnasium constructed. It was the best around. By that time, we had tuition students from surrounding towns. Basketball was very popular. Baseball, volleyball and track were popular, as were debating teams.

The gym stage served as a place for prize speaking, graduation activities, music presentations and plays. School dances were held there, too. Later, it became the place for the town and school meetings and still is the primary place for those. Before, that they were held in the Odd Fellows Hall.

Many of the things referred to in Hazel's account, I remember. When she mentions people using oil lamps and heating with wood or coal, it reminds me that my father was an electrician and plumber and changed many things for many people.

Fire in the Fasekis block changed the overall appearance of Main Street. Thankfully, the town Common remains central to the town and is wonderfully kept by the Parks and Recreation Department, as are the cemeteries.

Stepping back a few years, I must mention that skating on the Lamprey River was a favorite thing to do. The river was always frozen solid by November, and there would be a huge bonfire started. We also had a winter carnival and were happy to have a ski tow on Long Hill. We had sleds, double runners, toboggans and whatever made the sliding good.

Doctor Fernald was our local doctor, and I always remember that whether you went to his office or he came to your house, he had red medicine to prescribe.

The Second World War influenced all of us in various ways. In 1944, there were twenty graduates from high school. The classes remained much smaller for a few years after that as the guys went into the service. We became accustomed to food and gas rationing.

A trip to Manchester was a big event. Later, Andrew Gordon, who drove one of the school bus routes, started making weekly trips to Manchester on Thursdays. The other bus route was covered by Ai Welch.

Elm Street was lined with stores and everyone *did not* carry the exact same things. Our mall was the Montgomery Ward and Sears Roebuck catalogues. I preferred Sears, and if I knew my size, I could be assured that it would fit, unlike today. There were no big truck deliveries and everything came by train.

Mr. Blodgett, the high school shop teacher, also had a band (he played a saxophone). Dances were held at the barn near Onway Lake for several years. Later, a couple of neighboring towns held weekly dances in their halls, and many of us attended those.

We still debate local issues at the aforesaid town meetings. Everything will never be resolved to everyone's liking, but we hope to continue maintaining a pleasant community in which to reside.

I must add that those friends from the Orchard Street area, along with their spouses, have remained my close friends whether they still live in New England or are scattered across the country.

There is a road beside the Congregational Church, which we called Horse Shed Alley. It led to the depot. The ticket master was a local citizen named Judge Sanborn. There were benches inside where you could wait for the train. In that area, before getting to Main Street, was Whittier's Market, Reggie's Market and a public service company office. Continuing on to Main Street was Laura's restaurant, which served beer. We referred to it as the beer parlor. Past that was the bakery; Cy Smith's store; Bartlett's department store, which later became the White Cross Market (now the Senior Center); Mitchell's Barber Shop; and a gift shop attached to a very popular place called Candyland.

On the opposite side of Main Street there was Marcotte's fuel company, Asbury Small's store, the First National store, Hurd's Drugstore, the A&P store, Raymond Fruit Store and a small lunchroom.

If you lived on the outskirts you either went uptown, downtown or to town and remembered your shopping list and told the clerks what you wanted.

Local farms, whether large or small, provided us with eggs, chicken, milk and pork. The first milk lady I remember was Flossie Thibeault, who came with a horse and wagon. The horse would go ahead of her and stop at the next house. Mr. Fowler came door to door selling fish. During World War II, rabbits were raised for eating.

If you grew up here, you most often remember it as being your home, about which fond memories remain.

Remembrances of the '50s

By Sally Paradis

SUMMER

Summer always held a certain amount of excitement. Growing up on Orchard Street, it meant visits with my friend Carol and playing the new game of Canasta with Addie, nurse and housekeeper to Dr. Fred Fernald. We were served orange junket and other delicacies. After the doctor's office hours were over, we sat on the porch and kept an eye on the comings and goings of everyone uptown, and eventually gravitated to Candyland for a cherry Coke or a sumptuous Se-Sa-Ma-Ca (a scoop of vanilla ice cream, marshmallow sauce and chocolate sauce, topped with a generous handful of salted peanuts).

Summer heralded swimming at Swain's beach on Onway Lake, next to Camp Onway owned by the BSA Essex Council of Lawrence, Massachusetts. Each year brought new acquaintances, as camp counselors would sneak over when their charges were napping and visit the local girls. These well-mannered young men often attended local dances at school and were not held in great favor by some of the locals.

Summer arrived on Long Hill when a couple of events occurred. The first was the Ford station wagon from Pennsylvania making its way up the hill, loaded to the roof with luggage and Susan B. Hutchinson, signaling that another season of the summer theater was underway. Actors and directors descended from NYC, but Susan B. called on local handymen to keep the theater in good working order and repair. She also enlisted Raymond and area actors. It was good theater, producing shows playing on Broadway. People came from miles around, driving their shiny automobiles over the narrow dirt road to sit in the wooden chairs of different heights to enjoy "summer stock" that ranked among the best in New Hampshire. Every season concluded with one of William Shakespeare's plays, replete with beautiful sets and gorgeous costumes. [As an aside, Sally, at age twelve, played Louison in Molière's *Imaginary Invalid* and starred with her brother in Thornton Wilder's *Happy Journey*.] They had a "lock" on the punch concession served at intermission on the porch. Their mother made the punch. God knows what was in it—tea and juices for sure, but the rest is anyone's guess.

The other event was the blue "beech" wagon creating a cloud of dust announcing the arrival of Margaret Huddleston Cross, from Utica, New York, heir of the Tucker clan. She "summered" at the Browsing, summer home of Margaret's step-grandfather, Gilman Tucker. Margaret, in the long line of the Tucker family, had inherited most of the easterly acreage on the Long Hill and, throughout her life, sold most of this to friends.

Summer meant a job babysitting for our next-door neighbor's (the high school English/French teacher) little daughter, Paula. The first real job was at Holt's Department Store at fifty cents an hour, earning enough money for new school clothes.

SCHOOL

I could not wait to get to school each day. I enjoyed learning and all the activities it provided. Freshman classes don't get a chance to shine a lot, but the class of '58 held the first "Heart Hop" that netted big bucks, featuring Don Tibbetts, New Hampshire's biggest DJ name. (My friend Carol was crowned queen—who else? She was stunning and still is.)

The magical moment in February 1955 long remembered was when the RHS boys' basketball team was crowned Class B state champions. This small group, composed mostly of the class of 1955, since their elementary days were primed by Principal John Callaghan. Coach Wilbur Hixon took them all the way to the top with the final game being play in front of a packed house at UNH in Durham. Called a "Cinderella team" by sports writers all over New England, Raymond had petitioned the NHIAA to go from Class C (small schools) to Class B (medium schools) and competed with the likes of Exeter, Hampton and Salem. The "glow" has remained for all who were part of the scene to this day, including this freshman cheerleader.

Other remembrances? Playing in the school Drum and Bugle Corps during summers and capturing Eddie Fisher's autograph at Gill Stadium in Manchester where he was the star attraction for an event come to mind. The 1956 performance of Fred Waring's arrangement of the "Battle Hymn of the Republic" at the May concert under the direction of BU professor Dr. Warren Freeman bringing choral music to a new level at RHS, also stands out.

HOME

Mother and father were active in the community. Dinner-table conversation centered on happenings in town that day, with politics and the shoe factory at the top of the list. I remember running uptown after school to attend town meetings in the IOOF building, wood stove blazing, listening to the orators of the day, i.e., Fox, Eccleston, Guptill, Gordon and Hammond to name a few.

RADIO AND TV

I woke up each morning to Walter Winchell "and all the ships at sea" at 7:00 a.m. I listened to *The Lone Ranger*, *The Shadow*, *Fibber McGee and Molly* and much more. Then came television. I first saw one in the window of Eli Marcotte's store in 1948. Aunt Pearl and Uncle Bob Eccleston had one of the first sets in town; we had a front-row seat in their living room most nights: Uncle Miltie on Tuesday, *I Remember Mama* on Friday, Jackie Gleason, Sid Caesar on Saturday and, best of all, *I Love Lucy*. Mother and Dad finally bought a TV in time for the 1952 Democrat and Republican conventions that produced candidates Eisenhower and Stevenson. Life would never be the same again, but entertainment featured on endless channels today fall far short of what entertainment was like in the '50s on television.

CHURCH

I remember inging in the Methodist and combined choirs when Methodist and Congregational churches "yoked" for a period of time in the '50s. Georgina Smith was the organist, and Marion Guinea was the choir director. Mrs. Guinea gave piano lessons in her home on Orchard Street and several promising musicians got their starts with her. After her death, her upright concert grand piano was used by the church and still remains behind the altar of the Congregational Church, having been replaced with a modern "electronic" piano when the pipe organ is not in use.

How lucky we were to have grown up in this small town of Raymond, New Hampshire, in the '50s. Many friendships made still abide sixty years later.

20

FAMILY SKETCHES

John S. "Jack" Barnes Jr.

John S. Barnes Jr. was born August 21, 1931, in Arlington, Massachusetts. He attended Winchester High School and graduated from Manlius Military Academy in 1949.

After entering UNH in 1949, the Korean War was beginning and he decided to join the army. He was given an opportunity to study Russian and Chinese but averred he didn't want to spend his time eavesdropping on the enemy. He opted to go to Korea with a field artillery battalion.

He served on the front lines in 1951 and returned to the States in 1952. He reentered UNH and graduated in 1956. He met his wife, Frances, a native of Hudson, New Hampshire, at UNH.

Out of college and married, he worked for a time in Sarasota, Florida. Eventually, he joined McDonald's Corporation in Dedham, Massachusetts, in 1967.

In the mid-1970s, tired of traveling for McDonald's, he wanted to open his own McDonald's restaurant. He was given opportunities across the country, but opted for Raymond, where, he said, he would be nearer to Fenway Park.

As a UNH student, he had traveled from Fran's home in Litchfield to Durham and had driven the little-used "shortcut" known as Freetown

Road, passing Day's Potato Chip factory. Freetown Road was then a narrow, winding path connecting Route 102 to what is now Route 27, then Route 101. At that time, Route 102 passed through Raymond Village to connect to 101.

So he was familiar with the Raymond area, and moved here in 1978 to build the McDonald's restaurant, and this was to be his permanent home.

Always well-informed and interested in politics, he ran for selectman in 1985, and later in 1985, he was elected to the New Hampshire House. Elected to the New Hampshire Senate in 1992, he served four terms and was senate Majority Leader in 1998. He took a two-year hiatus in 1999 and 2000 but was reelected in 2002. He was reelected four more times until his retirement at the end of the 2011–12 legislative session.

Jack and Fran have two sons, Dwight and Warren, and a daughter, Susan Frances

Sally Paradis

I know of no living person who has been as constant in community involvement as has Sally Paradis.

Many people come and go in Raymond, after serving on boards, committees, in politics and various endeavors that bring some fleeting prominence, but eventually many find their way to other things, perhaps even other places.

Sally Guptill Paradis is descended from two old Raymond families, the Poors and the Trues. Two of Raymond's remaining old homes were built by these families in the area of town known as the Branch District. Asa Poor's granddaughter, Lizzie True, married George H. Guptill, MD, Raymond physician, whose son, George (Sally's father) married Mildred Adams of Deerfield. Sally was born in 1940. (Older brother, George Jr., an insurance executive for most of his life, has maintained close ties and a keen interest in his hometown.) Theirs was a household where interest in town politics held sway on a daily basis.

An RHS graduate, class of 1958, Sally attended Hesser Business College, where she met her husband, Roger. Married in 1960, they have one daughter, Jane, a 1993 UNH graduate.

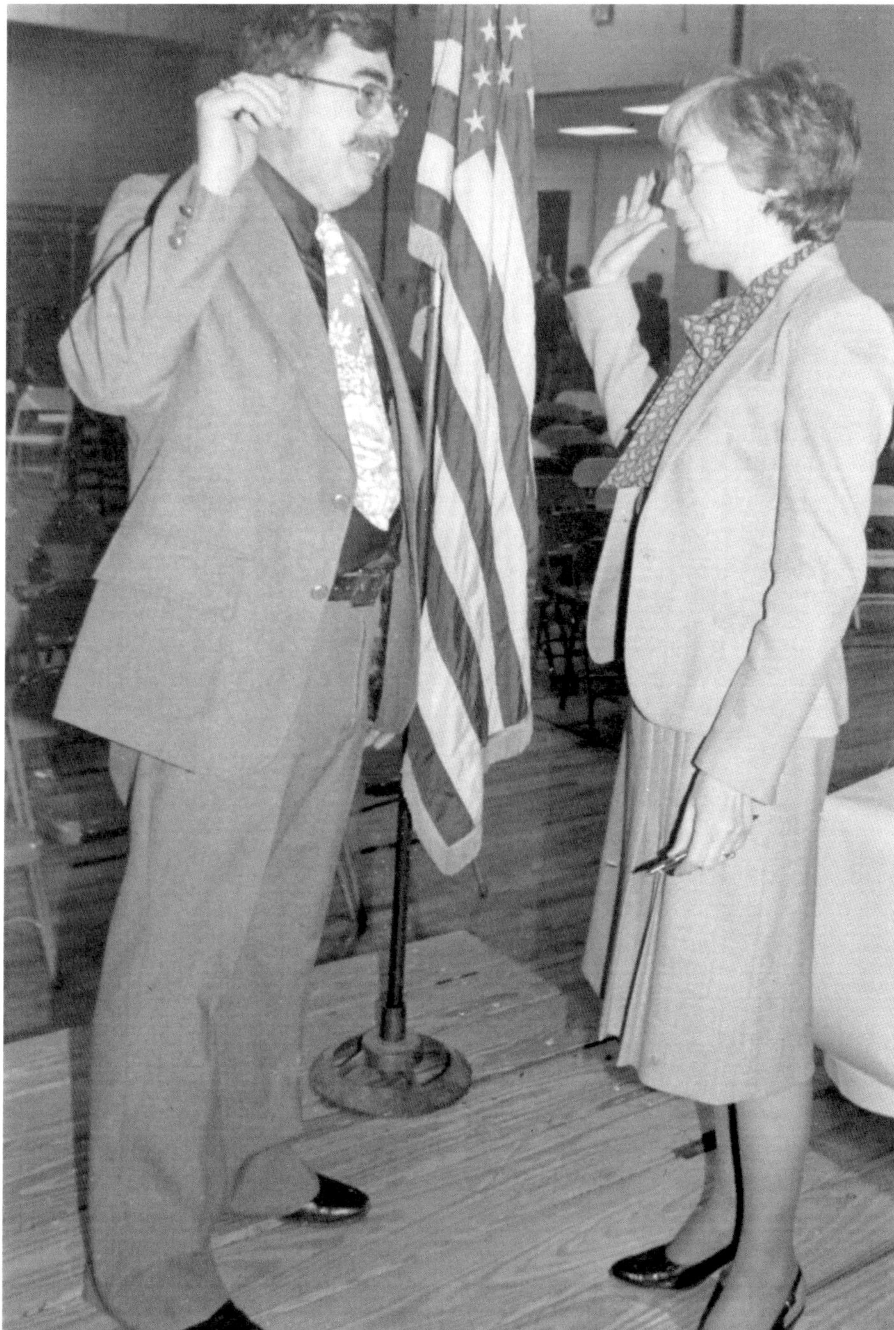

Moderator Frank Case swearing in the first female selectman, Sally Paradis. *Courtesy of Diana Dawes.*

Sally's interest in her community began when she served on the Pawtuckaway Co-operative Study Committee in the mid-'60s, followed by membership on the local school board from 1968 to 1980. After a term on the Municipal Budget Committee, she was elected and served on the board of selectmen from 1983 to 1993.

She co-chaired the town's 225th Celebration Committee with Ted Welch and, with others, headed an effort to erect memorials to World War II, Korean Conflict and Vietnam veterans. Another term on the Municipal Budget Committee and Historic District Commission followed.

With other RHS alumni, her interest turned to reviving the RHS Alumni Association (defunct since the mid-'60s) beginning with Homecoming 2000.

Following retirement in 2004, after forty-two years as an administrative assistant to eight school superintendents in neighboring communities, she filled out a two-year term on the school board, serving as building chair during construction of the IHGMS in 2005–06. After a fifty-year hiatus, she returned to the choir at the Congregational Church, served on the Restoration Committee in 2007–09 and continues to be church moderator.

She currently serves on the fundraising committee for the refurbishment of the Raymond Historical Society's 1892 depot in honor of the town's 250th celebration.

Wayne Welch

As I write this, Wayne Welch is a selectman and also the chairman of the 250th anniversary committee. The Welch family has been an entrepreneurial one for at least a century.

Wayne was born on January 20, 1954, to Frederick "Ted" Welch and Joan Howard. Ted's father was Ai S. Welch who operated the oil company Ai Welch & Sons. The rather unusual name "Ai," incidentally, is a biblical one.

Ai married Josephine Fernald, daughter of Dr. Fred Fernald, a well-known physician from Nottingham who had an office in Raymond. Dr. Fernald delivered a lot of babies, patched them up when they got hurt, vaccinated them and made house calls when they were sick. (As an aside, he didn't deliver me as he was a half-hour late, but I was told he tied my umbilical cord. I don't remember the incident.)

The Fernalds were descended from Revolutionary War luminaries General Joseph Cilley and Henry Dearborn, later a secretary of war.

Ai was a selectman and, during the late 1940s and early '50s, was voted most popular Raymond citizen in the high school yearbook.

In addition to selling home heating fuels, the Welches operated the school bus service for many years.

The Welch "complex," three buildings containing the Welch residence, the barn-office-business and the apartment building that was once the Riverview Hotel, was left to Ai's father, Frank Welch, from his father, who died young.

Frank Welch was married to Fannie Batchelder who was descended from an early Raymond family.

Frank's son, Ai, was born in 1899, and he and Josephine had seven children: Frederick (Ted), Josephine (Ardell), Neal, John, Joseph, Elizabeth and Alison.

Ted and Joan's children, including Wayne, were Steve, Ellen, Beverly, Paul, Jane and Bruce.

Wayne married Kathleen Cash, and they had Therren and Lindsey.

Wayne purchased Radio Grove Hardware from Paul O'Neil of Deerfield in 1997. He won his first stint as selectman in 2000 as a write-in.

Wayne's uncle Joe Welch tells a story about Ai concerning his heating oil account book. During the heating season, a lot of people couldn't pay their full bill and were trusted to make partial payments, and sometimes payment was very slow. I can recall my mother being most grateful toward the Welches for their forbearance.

Up until the 1960s, there were few checking accounts and no credit cards. People who worked in the shoe factory were paid on Thursday or Friday in cash in a little brown envelope. Part of the pay would be spent on the way home at the First National or A&P. Some stores ran a monthly account and bills would be paid in cash. The electric bill was paid at the Fruit Store in cash; the telephone bill (if one had a telephone) was paid at the telephone office, in cash.

Honorable Mention

As the lead author of this book, I get to make the call as to whom to profile as important citizens of Raymond, with the knowledge that there are hundreds more who make a community what it is. We are, however, limited by our publisher to a certain number of words.

Here is a sampling:

Kathleen Hoelzel, longtime town moderator, state representative, former school board and budget committee member; Tim Louis, longtime school district moderator, former HDC and budget committee member, who with wife Peg served as school board member and trustee of trust funds; Sandra Ellis, long service on the school board and budget committee; Edward French, selectman, school board member, budget committee member, school district treasurer; Franklin Bishop, state representative, selectman and conservation commission; and Lyman "Buster" Hammond, with his father Lyman Sr., heads a dynasty of elected road agents who kept the roads clear in the winter and smooth in the summer. Bless them all. We could write another book about these and departed icons of our "Fair Raymond."

21

CLOSING COMMENTS: FROM COWS TO SHOES TO DISTRIBUTION CENTER

Other than the inevitable discomforts of the aging process, this writer is grateful for the opportunity he's had to observe a relatively wide period in a community's life.

In my early childhood, agriculture was still the dominant occupation of many. A few subsistence farmers were still using horses to plow fields and haul carts and wagons. Cows were driven out to pasture in the morning, sometimes along the roads, and driven home at night. It was common to hear cowbells clanking from somewhere off in the woods.

World War II seemed to be the agent of change. There was still some dairying

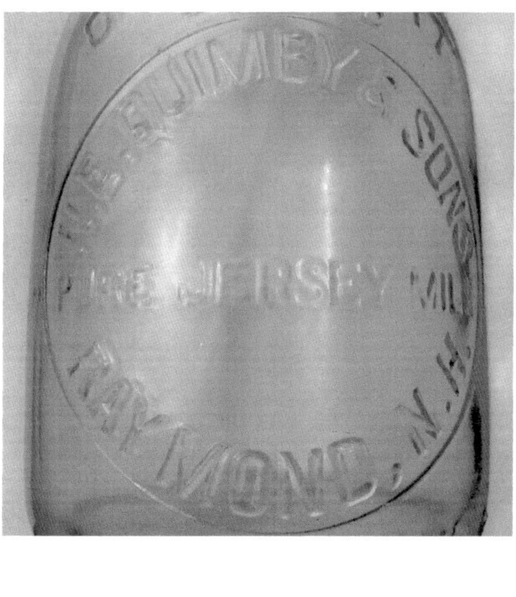

Agricultural days: "W.E. Quimby & Sons—Pure Jersey Milk—Raymond, NH." *Courtesy of Paul Brown.*

activity, but most farming became unnecessary with the transportation of produce on better highways with modern vehicles.

The manufactories in Raymond had a few good years with Bourque Shoe Company (becoming "Berk" Shoe, then Harman Shoe, and constructing a modern building) and the Falconer Shoe Company giving way to Regis Tanning Company.

Those manufacturers are long gone. The highways are the conduits for commuting miles away, and Raymond has become a central location for what is believed to be the largest single-story building in New Hampshire, the Walmart Distribution Center.

GRG

John McDaniels, RHS '52, has some impressive credentials. He graduated from Brown University and Yale Law School, was an officer in the U.S. Navy and had a career in international law and banking. He is now retired but stays busy helping Raymond's students. In high school, he was my age but a grade ahead of me, at least a head taller and considerably more mature. He was also a talented athlete who lettered in basketball at Brown and was inducted into the RHS Athletic Hall of Fame in 2006. His remarks on that occasion capture the essence of Raymond's heart and soul. An excerpt follows:

> *Recently I said to our daughter, Andrea, that I had not spent much time in Raymond. She replied: "Wait a minute; Raymond to you isn't a place, it's a state of mind. You're in Raymond all the time. You're talking about it all the time with us." She was referring to my sharing things that Bill Hurd said and stories of the Moulton brothers, George and Grover (father of Ed, mentioned earlier this evening) and their homemade baseball bats. George Gove was very helpful to me growing up. I have passed on endless words of wisdom from such people. And, the jokes that went around—from Mitchell's Barber Shop—I still am telling some of them to my family for the first time fifty-five years after I first heard them. They're a bit salty, but they're not bad.*
>
> *Andrea is right that Raymond has been a state of mind for me. It is important in the way I lead my life.*

Some of you may have known Charlie ("Casey") Rollins who died recently. When it happened, I sent an email from Switzerland to Pamela, his daughter, and Dan, his son (my niece and nephew). I said the sort of things one says in such situations and concluded by saying "he was a Good Raymond Guy." Dan replied saying: "Yes, you're right. He was the kind of guy who would spend all day Saturday for a neighbor he didn't know well, getting a lawn mower to work, even though it was a model he had never seen before. Good Raymond Guys do things like that."

There are a lot of Good Raymond Guys and Gals in this room right now. You understand what I am talking about. A Good Raymond Guy is someone who is straightforward, honest, works hard and is reluctant to take "no" for an answer. He has a good sense of humor (that may sometimes be at one end of the color spectrum). He occasionally pokes fun at himself.

John Callaghan reminded me recently (as he frequently does of things that happened fifty to sixty years ago) of that very forgettable speech at my graduation which was on the subject of sportsmanship, a typical subject for a jock. At the end of the speech I quoted Grantland Rice, a well-known sportswriter of that era: "When the one great scorer comes to write against your name, he cares not that you won or lost but how you played the game."

Well, I am getting a little closer to that guy with the score book. I'd be very pleased if he would say: "He was a Good Raymond Guy."

INDEX

ABOUT THE AUTHOR

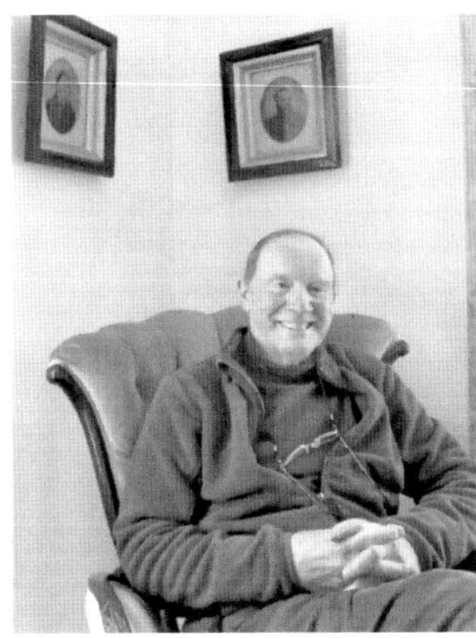

Paul Brown is a native of Raymond, New Hampshire, living in a home in which he was raised and about two hundred yards from the farmhouse in which he was born.

He is a tenth generation of both paternal and maternal families who are natives of the Granite State, which heritage has kindled his appreciation of its history from childhood.

Twice elected to the New Hampshire House of Representatives, he claims the "longest snooze" between legislative sessions, some forty-four years. In 2012, he was honored as "Legislator of the Year" by the New Hampshire Liberty Alliance.

He served a term on the town's board of selectmen and on several committees.

He is self-employed as a real estate appraiser, is married to Sheila, lives on a dirt road in an antique home and is the father of two children, two grandchildren and one great-granddaughter.